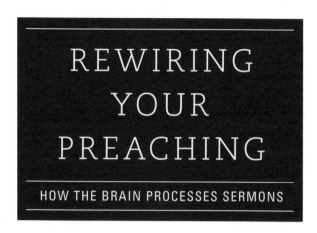

REWIRING
YOUR
PREACHING

HOW THE BRAIN PROCESSES SERMONS

RICHARD H. COX

IVP Books

An imprint of InterVarsity Press
Downers Grove, Illinois

InterVarsity Press
P.O. Box 1400, Downers Grove, IL 60515-1426
World Wide Web: www.ivpress.com
Email: email@ivpress.com

InterVarsity Press® is the book-publishing division of InterVarsity Christian Fellowship/USA®, a
movement of students and faculty active on campus at hundreds of universities, colleges and schools of
nursing in the United States of America, and a member movement of the International Fellowship of
Evangelical Students. For information about local and regional activities, write Public Relations Dept.,
InterVarsity Christian Fellowship/USA, 6400 Schroeder Rd., P.O. Box 7895, Madison, WI 53707-7895,
or visit the IVCF website at <www.intervarsity.org>.

Scripture quotations, unless otherwise noted, are from the New Revised Standard Version of the Bible,
copyright 1989 by the Division of Christian Education of the National Council of the Churches of Christ
in the USA. Used by permission. All rights reserved.

While all stories in this book are true, some names and identifying information in this book have been
changed to protect the privacy of the individuals involved.

Cover design: Cindy Kiple
Images: brain: © Sveta Demidoff/iStockphoto
        microphone: © apartment/iStockphoto
Interior design: Beth Hagenberg

ISBN 978-0-8308-4101-1

Printed in the United States of America ∞

Library of Congress Cataloging-in-Publication Data
A catalog record for this book is available from the Library of Congress.

P   18   17   16   15   14   13   12   11   10   9   8   7   6   5   4   3   2   1

Y   27   26   25   24   23   22   21   20   19   18   17   16   15   14   13   12

To

Betty Lou,
high school sweetheart and wife for life;

Dr. Vernon C. Grounds,
preacher par excellence and lifelong mentor;

the many great preachers
who have preached to me
and taught me how
to preach;

and those who continue to listen to me.

Contents

Foreword 9

Chapter Synopses 11

Preface 17

1. A Brainstorm Versus a Short Circuit 23

2. Linking Brain and Sermon 31

3. The Brain Sees Preaching as Unique 49

4. The Brain Uses Preaching for Healing 61

5. The Core Process of Preaching Is Brain Work . . . 71

6. Preaching Provides Brain Energy 79

7. Brain Stimuli Produce Behavioral Responses 89

8. Preaching and Pastoring Are Different 97

9. Getting to the Brain with Theology 108

10. Preaching and the Brain in Pain 129

11. Brain Healing and the Soul 133

12. Brain Healing and the Mind 146

13. Brain Healing and the Body 153

14. Brain Healing and the Community 159

Dénouement and Benediction 171

Acknowledgments 173

Appendix: *Checklist for Sermon Preparation* 175

Notes 177

Foreword

Why should those preaching today be interested in the brain? Surely preachers are about the business of saving and nurturing persons, not brains. Something special happened to those listening to Peter on the day of Pentecost: "Now when they heard this, they were cut to the heart" (Acts 2:37). We might ask, "What's new? People were cut to the heart then and they are cut to the heart now. The brain is simply a transmitter that moves the message to the heart and soul of the person."

Not so fast. Transport Peter to the present and place him on a stand in Times Square. Other than speaking to a more secular audience, the modern-day Peter must understand what is now basic to the neurosciences. First, the sensory organs gather the words of Peter, filter them, and move them forward to higher (and lower) levels of the brain, a brain that is far more than a transmitter. This brain, altered through the exposure to our very complex modern environment, attempts to make sense of the surrounding world. Peter must compete with shortened attention spans and with distractions that include smartphones, tablets, massive flat-screen monitors and a pace of life that is dramatically faster than in Jerusalem. We don't know the length of Peter's sermon, but if it lasted even thirty minutes, an audience accustomed to fifteen-second sound bites would not linger for the punch line. If this is the end of the story, it is not an encouraging story for Peter or any would-be Peter in the twenty-first century.

Yet this is not the end of the story. The brain is no longer a complete mystery. We have learned much about this most complex of organs over the past one hundred years. For one (dating back to Freud but understood in far more detail today), the brain works constantly at levels other than consciousness. These workings of the brain, not noticed by the person, are not beyond our ability to study. We have learned what types of stimuli are muted by the brain and what types are recognized and enhanced before those stimuli ever reach the level of conscious thought. We have learned how recognition of different sounds can short-circuit consciousness and evoke visceral responses that often repel the listener and even surprise the listener in their intensity. We have learned much about short-term and long-term memory, most relevant to the "takeaway" message of the sermon.

Our growing understanding of how the brain works can be a means to uncovering the desired goal of those who deliver a sermon, but it should never be considered the end product of the sermon. Sermons can change brains (Cox correctly emphasizes the plasticity of the brain), yet the purpose of the sermon is not to change brains but rather to change persons. The essence of personhood supervenes on the brain. In other words, the brain is necessary but not sufficient for personhood. At the interface of the person with his or her God rests the mystery of the sermon. The sermon is carried by the Spirit to the person via the brain, not to the brain via the person. And within this spirit, Richard Cox expertly and passionately exhorts those who occupy the pulpit to acquire the knowledge and skills from the brain sciences that can inform and shape their sermons. He clearly has worked diligently and effectively to do the same.

Dan G. Blazer, MD, PhD
J. P. Gibbons Professor of Psychiatry and Behavioral Sciences
Duke University Medical Center
Durham, North Carolina

Chapter Synopses

Educating the mind without educating the heart is no education at all.

ARISTOTLE

Preaching to the mind while disregarding the heart is to preach in vain; and preaching to the heart while disregarding the mind is equally of no gain.

R. COX

CHAPTER 1: A BRAINSTORM VERSUS A SHORT CIRCUIT

When vibrations hit the eardrum, they are not words, only sounds; the brain can enter into confusion or synthesis. The ability of the speaker to *religare*—that is, attach new learning to old—makes the difference. Otherwise, information has no meaning and the human brain enters into a process of rejection. It is imperative to understand how the brain "hears," then "translates" and then decides what to do with new information.

CHAPTER 2: LINKING BRAIN AND SERMON

The thinking part of the body is the brain. It has special neural pathways that allow the hearer to accept or reject verbal stimuli. Preaching must address listeners and stimulate the knowledge of those brain-wired processes if it is to be "heard."

CHAPTER 3: THE BRAIN SEES PREACHING AS UNIQUE

There is nothing comparable to a sermon. A religious service is the only venue in which a talk is called a sermon or homily. No other organization presents truth from a pulpit in the same fashion as the church. From infancy, the human brain is conditioned to see the minister and what he or she says as unique and demanding of respect.

CHAPTER 4: THE BRAIN USES PREACHING FOR HEALING

The human brain is constantly looking for integration, synthesis, pleasure and hope. Nothing offers these possibilities more unconditionally than preaching. The mind is healed and relationships are healed, while emotional pain and despair are replaced with hope and peace. There is now scientific evidence supporting this. Faith, which is the basis for spiritual healing, is enhanced, encouraged and modeled with brain-based preaching.

CHAPTER 5: THE CORE PROCESS OF PREACHING IS BRAIN WORK

Preaching allows the brain to rethink, reorganize, reconnect and reconstruct itself into new neurological pathways, which is an incredibly complicated process. Neuroscience has shown us how the brain literally retrains itself in new ways of thinking. This process is called neuroplasticity. Preaching offers the possibility for the brain actually to change itself—not just in thinking but in anatomy.

CHAPTER 6: PREACHING PROVIDES BRAIN ENERGY

Brain energy comes not only from food and drink, but also from what we think, the environment, the symbols that surround us and the company we keep. Preaching in a sanctuary surrounded by symbols provides an environment that unconsciously ties us to values and beliefs, words that enforce the environment and a congregation of persons who reinforce the entire context. These are powerful sources of brain energy. Recent neurological findings support these statements.

CHAPTER 7: BRAIN STIMULI PRODUCE BEHAVIORAL RESPONSES

It isn't possible for the brain to receive external stimuli without producing a behavioral response. The response may be to accept, to reject, to file away for future reference or to make immediate decisions. How we behave is based on what we believe, and what we believe is based on what we already believe plus new stimuli. All behavior is purposeful because all behavior is based on belief, and belief drives behavior.

CHAPTER 8: PREACHING AND PASTORING ARE DIFFERENT

Being a good preacher and being an effective pastor are very different; they require different skills, and yet they support each other. Effective preaching is the foundation for successful pastoring, and being an effective pastor prepares listeners to "hear" the preaching.

CHAPTER 9: GETTING TO THE BRAIN WITH THEOLOGY

Theology is unique in that everyone believes—or believes not to believe. The brain is energized with effective preaching and thrown into debate with itself. The neural pathways of memory are activated, while the cortex and social/behavioral parts of the brain are stimulated and forced to deal with new and old information. There are few other bodies of knowledge that excite, stimulate, anger and appease all at the same time.

CHAPTER 10: PREACHING AND THE BRAIN IN PAIN

With scientific accuracy, technologies such as MRIs have shown how the brain responds favorably to information that offers hope, peace and tranquility. Electroencephalogram records have shown brain-wave amplitude and type to change with various verbal inputs, such as preaching styles.

CHAPTER 11: BRAIN HEALING AND THE SOUL

Soul pain is real; numerous respected medical and psychological experts attest to the fact that when the brain is in turmoil, the body does not heal as well. And when the soul (even for those who reject the idea of a soul) finds healing—some call it forgiveness or catharsis—the body and mind work together to heal each other.

CHAPTER 12: BRAIN HEALING AND THE MIND

It has long been recognized that the thinking brain changes the way we act. The brain is a physical part of the anatomy; the mind is the soul that carries out the thinking of the brain. When the brain is sick, so are actions. If we are to change people's actions, we must first heal their brains. New science tells us about neuroplasticity—the ability of the brain to rewire itself and thus restore the mind.

CHAPTER 13: BRAIN HEALING AND THE BODY

The body can't be separated from the brain. Psychosomatic medicine offered philosophies and a psychology of body-mind illness, even before the time of Freud. The brain produces neural connections that support or discourage neuroconnections, neurotransmitters and neural energy for the body either to stay sick or to get well. Preaching can play a vital part in allowing and helping the mind as a positive reinforcing agent for mental and physical health.

CHAPTER 14: BRAIN HEALING AND THE COMMUNITY

As old as the book of Proverbs is the statement "As a person thinks, so shall he be." The community can heal only as our brains are rewired to rethink how the values we say we hold apply to the larger self. Communities and nations, just like individuals and organizations, have distinct personalities. These community personalities also inherit and develop their own sociological and spiritual illnesses. There is no place on earth where community healing can be more singly affected and empowered than in a pulpit, through a sermon.

DÉNOUEMENT AND BENEDICTION

A dénouement is not an ending but a blessing on a beginning. So it is with the sermon and with this book. The purpose is to give not a completion but a challenge that can't be ignored.

Preface

Science without religion is lame. Religion without science is blind.

ALBERT EINSTEIN (1941)

Every minister wonders about the effectiveness of his or her weekly sermons. With some parishioners barely awake, others daydreaming, parents attending to infants and only a few in sacrosanct reflection, it's anybody's guess what is going on in the minds of those sitting in the pews. What are they *hearing*, or are they just *listening* with their brains focused elsewhere? While these questions are not new and have been asked many times, modern neuroscience has shed sufficient light on them to confirm our suspicions. The good news is that discoveries from neuroscience can equip the preacher with more knowledge to engage brains, minds and bodies, so that those in the congregation are more likely to profit from the sermons.

Every preacher's challenge today is *attracting* new attendees and *retaining* them. Though preachers would like to attract new members, most would just settle for more people to attend services. It's a new day for preachers and for congregations. In some denominations, full-time pastors are being replaced by part-time and even lay ministers. Church buildings are going into disrepair. Many congregations are too small to stay viable, so they close. Others merge only to find they no longer really exist. Ministers and congregations are attempting every conceivable heroic attempt to stay open, even if barely alive. For example, the *Platsburg* (Vermont) *News* reported on December 8, 2009, that the First Baptist Church's Tiffany stained-glass window was for sale due to the need for funds to stay afloat. Offerings, bake sales and ice cream socials no longer provide the needed funds. Some pastors produce psychosocially appealing sermons, hoping not to upset the saints too severely, and even entertain them a bit, and to appeal to the unchurched.

So we have a problem. Is there an answer? Would powerful, purposeful preaching save the day? It's hard to say, but it's not hard to see that without such preaching, simply keeping the doors open does not fulfill the church's purpose. Without powerful preaching, is caring for the poor and feeding the hungry sufficient to make the church more than the United Way or Red Cross?

It must be added quickly that the church's ministries are primary to Christian mission, but it is legitimate to ask, "What is the church without the preached Word?" Would a community respond to the kind of powerful, purposeful preaching that characterized the churches of yesteryear? Many great churches have been built on powerful preaching. Could it work again?

Preaching that is both Christocentric and neuropsychologically sound is powerful. New knowledge is available on how the brain hears and processes information into decisions and resultant activity. Even elementary neurobiological knowledge can help every preacher to think and preach *intentionally*. While much preaching is done conscientiously, the results are often incidental and accidental rather than intentional. By adding intentional knowledge and purpose to the mix, much more can be accomplished.

This book may be considered a call to purposeful preaching—taking advantage of the latest neuroscientific knowledge, coupled with the power of the gospel and the energy of the Holy Spirit.

Utilizing new knowledge about how we learn and how the brain translates words into decisions and then into actions should invigorate those who have the ears of so many people each week. *The psychological and neurobiological fields have raised the bar on our understanding of how preaching can be done and how sermons are received and interpreted by the brain.* Intentional, purposeful preaching can actually produce new neural pathways that cause the brain to change the way it thinks and how its owner acts.

This is not a textbook on neuroscience or a discourse on neurotheology. It's a book to help those who preach to understand how their words are translated into meaning, meaning into decision, and decision into action. It doesn't seek to determine whether the brain is wired for spirituality. We now know it is, based on the research of numerous neuroscientists, such as Andrew Newberg, who documents it in his book *How God Changes Your Brain* (Ballantine, 2009), and Bruce Lipton in *The Biology of Belief* (Elite Books, 2005). These are only two famous neuroscientists who have dispelled any notion that the brain is spiritually neutral.

This book postulates that knowledge of how the brain works will enable preachers to be more effective. Further, we must differentiate *neurobiology* from *neurotheology*. Neuroscience is based on research findings and seeks to verify anatomical and functional reality. Neurotheology seeks to validate an anatomical basis of belief and is based on philosophical assumptions.

Neurotheology tends to be reductionist, reducing faith to the physiological mechanism of the human brain—that is, it is an anatomical/physiological philosophy of religion. However, neuroscience proves increasingly that the hand of God is continuously at work *in* and *on* the human brain. Neurobiology provides an understanding of *how* and *why* the brain is capable of learning and believing. These disciplines are sufficiently complex as to require many volumes to explain; therefore, it can't and need not be done here.

However, it's imperative to understand the differences between the two approaches. Neurotheology is physically grounded and attempts to prove that somehow humans are biologically connected to the spiritual. Neurobiology does not address *what* the brain believes, but explains the process of *how* it assimilates and stores information for use. This latter knowledge is most helpful to preachers, and this book is written based on its assumptions.

Rewiring Your Preaching is not an exploration of the neuroscience of faith, but of how the *knowledge* of neuroscience *enables* faith. The hope is that we can gain sufficient understanding to provide an elementary grounding and deep respect for how God uses our brains in the journey of faith. Hopefully, this writing is "preacher friendly" and does not disgrace either theology or the neurosciences. A claim is made not for the intricate accuracies of neuroscience or for a sophisticated depth of theology, but rather for the accuracy of an application of what we know about how the brain works and its relevance to translating spoken word into meaning and meaning into discipleship.

Today's preaching calls for the widest and deepest knowledge that preachers can attain—and in as many disciplines as possible. Congregations in this century are, for the most part, highly educated and expect a level of intellectual acumen, vastly more than in former years. A thorough knowledge of theology is a given; however, also knowing how the brain works can greatly impact the effectiveness of sermons.

Preachers today are expected to be conversant in many disciplines. With modern-day technology, multidisciplinary information is now in the public domain. It was a different time in history when many of our predecessors preached. Less education was required, and there was considerably less information in the public domain. As we know from history, there was a time when only the clergy had access to the Bible itself. The common person was unable to read and write until relatively recently. As recently as in Spurgeon's time and Wesley's time, for instance, the average congregant had less education than the minister; many had little or no schooling. This is no longer the case. Worshipers are highly educated—some to a greater extent than their clergy, albeit in different disciplines.

Just as the minister expects the physician to possess greater knowledge than the patient, the congregant expects greater knowledge from the clergy. In spite of the fact that in earlier times congregants had less formal education, the great theological teachers of the day recognized the need to use every tool possible and as much interdisciplinary knowledge as appropriate for great preaching.

Is such knowledge necessary? No, because God uses the Word with the gifts that each preacher brings to the pulpit. However, not possessing at least a fundamental understanding of how the brain works, when it is possible to do so, limits our ability and the power of the message we have. It is also possible to utilize modern neurobiological and neuropsychological knowledge in preaching without becoming a neuroscientist. The great preachers of the past attempted to be knowledgeable in a wide variety of disciplines and admonished their students to know the sciences—when far less was known than we know today. They did not see knowledge of the sciences and theology as antithetical or in any way disparate to preaching, but rather as complementary.

Many clergy have frowned on scientific knowledge, seeing it as a threat to faith—for which there has never been, nor will there ever be, scientific proof. Since it was suspect, they "threw the baby out with the bathwater" and failed to benefit from it. Two of the greats, Charles Haddon Spurgeon and John Wesley, are prime examples of recommending knowledge from the sciences. Spurgeon wrote,

> It seems to me that every student for the Christian ministry ought to know at least something of every science; he should intermeddle with every form of knowledge that may be useful in his life's work. God has made all things that are in the

world to be our teachers, and there is something to be learned from every one of them; . . . so he who does not learn from all things that God has made will never gather all the food that his soul needs, nor will he be likely to attain to that perfection of mental manhood which will enable him to be a fully-equipped teacher of others.[1]

Wesley expected that clergy would be well rounded in the arts and sciences, having a grasp of much more than theology. He painted a picture showing the importance of understanding human behavior, thinking and the application of all the arts and sciences in preaching. It's not a stretch to believe that if he were alive today, he would fully embrace the neurosciences, expect his students to study this field and incorporate this new knowledge into his art of preaching.

In his *Address to the Clergy*, Wesley spoke of the sciences and other knowledge, saying, "Some knowledge also is, to say the least, equally expedient."[2] He further admonished, "There is yet another branch of knowledge highly necessary for a Clergyman, and that is, knowledge of the world; a knowledge of men, of their maxims, tempers, and manners, such as they occur in real life."[3]

Every clergy person must ask in good conscience, "Who is listening, and if hearing, what is actually being heard, and what will come of it?"

Richard H. Cox

1

A Brainstorm Versus a Short Circuit

The results of preaching are predicated and dependent on the worshiper's neural (brain) ability to pay attention, integrate current thought with experiences and knowledge, and utilize memory. When vibrations hit the eardrum, they are not words, but only sounds. The brain can enter into either confusion or synthesis, depending on the ability of the speaker to *religare*—that is, attach new learning to old. Otherwise, information has no meaning and the human brain enters into a process of rejection.

It's imperative to understand how the brain "hears," then "translates," then decides what to do with new information. A later chapter will discuss the brain and mechanism of hearing in detail, but here it's important to understand the psychological ramifications of what we hear.

The brain, without any conscious intent, determines very early in a sermon whether the mind's lights will come on or will short out and turn off. The choice of words, the syntax, the pronunciation, the inflexion of the voice and much more will determine whether the brain decides to tune out or tune in. Although a brain is very different from a light switch, the result is the same. It takes only a nanosecond for a compromised light switch to short out and stop working. The same is true with those who listen to preachers, lecturers and teachers. A small child was asked, "What is the person called who continues to talk when the listener has stopped listening?" The child replied, "A teacher." An adult might have said, "A preacher."

Listeners either turn the lights off or keep them on, and they don't always consciously know that they're doing so. External stimuli often make this decision for us. Some people are capable of consciously using a kind of brain rheostat that brightens and lowers the light (attention mechanism), which doesn't allow enough illumination for them to see the picture correctly. This kind of intentionality is related to interest in the topic at hand, and at times in one's motivation to remember information being given. Others are unaware of the external forces acting upon them. Sometimes this is worse than no attention at all, since the listener has partial knowledge that may be misinterpreted and misapplied. A congregation that is half asleep may be worse than none at all. Although many factors affect the listener in the process of paying attention, the minister can control some, such as sermon structure, vocabulary and method of preaching.

The average Christian's belief about preaching is largely ethereal, meaning they believe that somehow people *automatically* decide what to do with what they hear. Others believe that there is no need to worry about the style of preaching, since all results are simply what "God wants to happen." There's no doubt that the ultimate results of preaching depend on the working of the Holy Spirit. The Scriptures are emphatic that God's word accomplishes his purposes: "So shall my word be that goes out from my mouth; it shall not return to me empty, but it shall accomplish that which I purpose, and succeed in the thing for which I sent it" (Is 55:11).

But because God is capable of blessing poor sermons is no excuse to preach poorly. Knowledge and tools now available from the neurosciences can assist us in more powerful and productive preaching, and they in no way diminish belief in the power of the

Holy Spirit, but rather magnify our ability to understand how God works through the physiology of the human brain. In medicine, we don't diminish God by further understanding the disease mechanism, nor do we lessen his power of healing. The same is true in understanding how the mind works and how preaching becomes effective.

Simply because a person hears does not mean that her or his brain is listening. We hear sounds all the time in traffic, on elevators and in restaurants but don't listen to them. Often we recognize their presence only when they are called to our attention. The same is true of the spoken word, whether in casual conversation or in sermons. Therefore, there may be many hearers present but few or no listeners.

The human learning process is one of listening, memory and integration. We receive information within the context of previous knowledge and process it through the filter of memory; then we decide what to do with it.

Listening uses memory to experience the past in the present and to bring the future into the present before its time. Memory coupled with new information, based on perceived need, is the engine that drives the brain to change. Preaching must build on past knowledge by bringing that knowledge into the present, coupling it with new information, and making it meaningful for our future need before we need it. Since we keep only core memory in our immediate consciousness (what is required for essential human function), all other memory is recalled and reconstructed with the additions and subtractions of newly configured information. Some of this recall takes nanoseconds, and some requires more time and additional cues to bring it into consciousness. New material may be considered "associated learning," because it is always added to previous knowledge that has been stored in various parts of the brain.

Neurochemical and neurophysiological activity determine whether new information will be given short-term status or will be cataloged for long-term storage. An area in the brain called the hippocampus is responsible for storing memory. Neural activity in the prefrontal cortex, striatum, limbic system and association cortex, along with many other brain structures, determine what information is stored, how it is integrated and whether or not it is worth dealing with at all.

The brain can't possibly remember every bit of information it receives. If it did, it would become overloaded very early in life. Some information is seen as extraneous and unnecessary. Other information is considered unnecessary at the time but can be revisited in the future, so it's cataloged and stored. And other information is considered important for immediate growth or survival.

Dr. Andrew Newberg, an acclaimed neuroscientist, and his associates at the University of Pennsylvania came to the following conclusions regarding religious ideation and the brain:

- Each part of the brain constructs a different perception of God.

- Every human brain assembles its perceptions of God in uniquely different ways, thus giving God different qualities of meaning and value.

- Spiritual practices, even when stripped of religious beliefs, enhance the neural functioning of the brain in ways that improve physical and emotional health.

- Intense, long-term contemplation of God and other spiritual values appears to permanently change the structure of those parts of the brain that control our moods, give rise to our conscious notions of self and shape our sensory perceptions of the world.

- Contemplative practices strengthen a specific neurological circuit that generates peacefulness, social awareness and compassion for others.[1]

Recent studies utilizing fMRI (functional magnetic resonance imaging) are very close to pinpointing specific anatomical locations for various kinds of thinking—even the location of various virtues. If this is accomplished, science will have invaded the very soul of the human—our inextricably interwoven mind and body. The implications for teaching and preaching are staggering. Preachers will continue to have the same duties, but accountability for reaching the mind will greatly increase when we know the mechanism causing words to become decisions. Institutions of higher learning with substantial academic credibility, such as Emory University, University of Florida, University of Illinois and California Institute of Technology, are among those on the forefront of these studies. The studies are preliminarily showing compassion to be located in the insula, along with sociability. Empathy and morality are believed to be in the amygdala, along with anger and rage. Meditation is likely in the angular gyrus.[2]

Newberg reports that there are "God circuits" in our brains. He credits the parietal-frontal circuit as establishing the "you and God" relationship and the frontal lobe as creating and integrating ideas about God. He believes the thalamus gives emotional meaning to concepts of God, and he credits an overstimulated amygdala for potentially causing frightening, authoritative, punitive ideas of God and suppressing the frontal lobe's ability to think logically about God. The striatum may allow a person to feel safe in the presence of God.[3]

As speculative as this may sound, there is enough solid evidence to attract many of our brightest neuroscientists. These scientists are spending countless hours and budgets to help us understand our spiritual selves. Preachers do not *need* this kind of proof, but it's great that modern science is testifying to biblical concepts that have been known for centuries.

How It Works Is Still a Mystery

Even though neuroscientific knowledge helps us to better understand the human thinking process, we need to be reminded that when (and if) pinpoint locations in the brain for spirituality are proven, we still will not know how it all works. We *will* know that we are "fearfully and wonderfully made" (Ps 139:14). It will still remind us that the "wind blows where it chooses, and you hear the sound of it, but you do not know where it comes from or where it goes. So it is with everyone who is born of the Spirit" (Jn 3:8-9). It was the Spirit of God that moved on the waters to create physical life (Gen 1:2), and it is the Spirit of God that continues to move on human minds to create spiritual life.

The mystery of how things work is necessary for faith and for the inherent dependence of humans on God. The apostle Paul wrote, "We speak of God's wisdom, secret and hidden, which God decreed before the ages for our glory . . . as it is written, 'What no eye has seen, nor ear heard, nor the human heart conceived'" (1 Cor 2:7, 9). It is not immoral to investigate the mystery, because in the investigation we discover the soul, depth and impenetrability of it, knowing that it is beyond our complete understanding. We do, however, gain limited understanding. Again, Paul seemed to understand this complexity of life: "For now we see in a mirror, dimly, but then we will see face to face. Now I know only in part; then I will know fully, even as I have been fully known" (1 Cor 13:12). The mystery is essential.

THE MIND IS EASILY TRICKED

An observation will help to illustrate just how easily the mind can fall prey to illusion and magic. There was a fireplace glowing in a hotel, with several people standing in front of it, warming their hands by the heat of a gas log emitting an imperceptible flame. In front of the fireplace was a stack of oak logs, fireplace tongs, a shovel, a poker and an ash bucket filled with old newspapers and pinecones. The tongs would not be used, the wood would not be burned, and the ash bucket would remain without ashes. But the ambience was not fake; the glow and the tiny flame were all real and gave a cozy feeling to the otherwise cold hotel lobby. The flame was imperceptible, but the ambience was real.

The brain is known for exchanging ambience for reality and vice versa. When this occurs, the body responds to the brain message in real time. In this instance, the small flame, fireplace tools and pile of wood connected the brain to previously embedded "truth" that "fireplace and flame" mean "warm." Although there was a small bit of warmth, the amount was not equal to one's perception. Exaggerated perception greatly modified the "truth." The ambience was indeed real, but something was missing—the truth.

The ambience was used to trick the mind into believing something that was not real and responding accordingly. So, thinking human beings responded in reality even when the environment was presented to them in fiction. Ambience brings us to accept something to be more than it actually is. It becomes a mental mirage; we "see" the wet road ahead and slow down, only to discover when arriving at the "sight" that it no longer exists, but has moved ahead by the same distance as when it was first "seen."

Perception is everything to the brain. A child who has been burned by a hot stove may avoid the stove even when it is cold, because the brain has been conditioned to believe that stoves are hot and burn. That child may also perceive that his or her knee is broken when it's only scraped in a fall. Perception is a combination of *fact* and *feeling*.

What does this have to do with preaching? Everything. Productive preaching requires both *fact* and *feeling*. The more "educated" churches tend to emphasize fact without feeling, and others are often just the opposite. For instance, many charismatic assemblies appear to operate primarily on feeling, while "university" churches may assiduously strive to avoid any appearance of being "feely." Of importance is the motivation behind these extremes. It appears that many believe that feeling always contaminates fact and that fact always contaminates feeling. When put into action, both philosophies lull people into adulterated truth or half-truth, spinning the gospel to fit the perceived need of the day and accommodating their biases. In these cases, we can be certain that the mind will become conditioned to whatever is preached and act accordingly. Ambience can be substituted for reality in theology too.

2

Linking Brain and Sermon

The thinking part of the body is the brain. It is filled with millions of special neural pathways that allow the hearer to accept or reject verbal stimuli. Preachers must utilize the knowledge of those brain-wired processes if they are to be "heard." They do not need to fully understand *how* the processes work, but must understand the methods of activating them.

Although we don't fully understand how the brain works and undoubtedly will never figure it out completely, this doesn't excuse us from utilizing every ounce of human knowledge for preaching the glory of God. Preachers, among all professionals, are persuaders of the mind by calling, training and professional identity. To ignore what we know that could make the task more efficient and productive would be to squander part of our modern stewardship—the stewardship of neuroscientific knowledge.

Have you ever wondered just what is going on inside the heads of your congregants while you're preaching? It's encouraging to know that it's impossible for sermons to go in one ear and out the other. The brain is incapable of ignoring external stimuli. It must deal with all stimuli in some way. Parishioners may appear to be just sitting there, but their brains are working diligently either attempting to dismiss or processing what is going on (it must even process stimuli to ignore it).

All brain activity requires brain energy. We must then ask, "How does the ear hear words, then translate them into ideas, then move ideas into decisions and decisions into actions?" It may be something like the age-old question "How does a brown cow eat green grass and produce white milk?" Neuroscience gives us some knowledge as to how the ear turns sound waves into brain thoughts that produce mental and physical action.

The brain mechanism is very much like the old-fashioned telephone switchboard. A person could call in on a line and be connected to many trunk lines at the same time—somewhat like a modern conference call. It was also possible to be on a party line in which many callers could listen in on a conversation—often uninvited. The spoken word comes to the "switchboard" (thalamus) and is connected to many "trunk lines" (striatum, limbic system, association cortex, motor cortex and so on) simultaneously. The incoming call must be acknowledged even to be ignored. The switchboard operator (in this case the brain's owner) must decide where to connect the incoming stimuli—in recognizing that it is to be ignored, put "on hold" or simply cut off. Stimuli to the brain can activate more than one area of the brain automatically, like the party line.

For those who are too young to know anything about a party line or a switchboard, we can use the analogy of the circuit breaker in an electrical fuse box. The spoken word (electricity) comes into the fuse box on one line and, depending on how many light switches are turned on around the house, lights up many lights and appliances. Or, like the party line, it will automatically energize any light or appliance that is already turned on. The intentional use of neurobiological knowledge can help the preacher to turn on the switches.

All Information Is Acted On

The brain selectively classifies information based on three premises: (1) preset needs, such as hormonal, metabolic and bodily function needs, (2) previous learning that determines the meaning of new information and (3) immediate emotional or physical needs that prepare for intellectual growth or for hormonal emergencies such as fright, flight or fight. New information is filtered faster than we can think and is immediately evaluated and sent to the part of the brain capable of managing that new knowledge.

When the brain receives new information, preset physiological and hormonal systems are immediately activated, some of which are simple reflex actions (such as a knee jerk). Others signal physiological mechanisms such as hunger, thirst, being too hot or too cold, or bodily movements such as the need to get out of the way of a moving vehicle. New information is reviewed, processed, cataloged and stored according to its importance at the moment and within the context of memory. In other words, what happens to new information that enters the brain is predicated and dependent on previously accepted and already stored information. What happens to this information depends on where in the brain it is stored. If it is cognitively acceptable to the brain, it is processed differently than if the brain decides it is cognitively dissonant.

Dissonant information is not necessarily discarded; it is processed differently than information that is consonant. Some new information may be interpreted by the brain as in need of immediate action, either physiologically or hormonally, or both. A sneeze or a cough may be interpreted as potentially threatening and requiring immediate action for self-preservation. Other new information may be interpreted as unnecessary and discarded (although rarely, since virtually all information is stored somewhere). Just as in a computer, wastebasket items may be recalled if the circumstances demand it. We must say "most" information, since the brain does not retain all information in a usable form. Also, as with any other wastebasket, sometimes if the information is needed, neuronal pathways are reactivated, although sometimes it takes some searching to locate the previously discarded information.

Words Alone Do Not Make Meaning

Preaching—that is, spoken words—requires a complex set of neural mechanisms. Spoken words (sound waves) are received by the outer ear until they reach the tympanic membrane (eardrum) from which the vibrations are conducted via three very tiny bones (ossicles) in the middle ear into the inner ear. The inner ear contains thousands of hair cells (the organ of Corti) that change the vibrations into electrical signals that are sent on to the brain by way of the eighth cranial nerve, the hearing nerve (one of twelve major nerves in the brain that serve the entire body).

At that point, the sounds carry only physical information; they have no higher intellectual value. Only when these signals are translated by the brain based on one or more of the three previously discussed premises do they become meaningful. That is, meaning is based on *general need, previous information* or *immediate survival need.* Repetition of stimuli within any of these methods creates automatic pathways for the acceptance, integration or rejection of new information. If properly prepared, the preacher is capable of helping *hearers* become *listeners* and assisting them in turning on the right switches for the best immediate action, delayed action, cognitive storage and integration for decision making.

Therefore, preaching is a major factor in building the structure for learning, especially learning required for spiritual growth. Although certainly a major function of the brain is to house, nourish and support the function of the central nervous system, most of the human cortex is related to higher-order processes such as interpretation, association and integration. It is to this larger part of the brain (interpretation, association and integration) that preaching is addressed.

Context Makes the Difference

The context and environment in which new information is received influences what will happen to new information. The soldier who becomes accustomed to gunshot blasts may later jump automatically when a car backfires. An individual may weep or laugh at an incident unrelated to her or him, due to associations with something that happened in her or his past.

Preaching is always within a context and an environment. The context is always larger and more inclusive than the message. The environment is usually a religious service of some sort. Neuroscience has shown that when new information is repeated continuously and sequentially, it produces changes both in the process of cognition and in the resultant thoughts.

Theologian Richard Lischner correctly asserted, "This church exists for the world, but it renews its identity when it gathers for worship. It speaks in the world, but it learns its 'distinctive talk' when its members come together around word and sacrament."[1] Within this environment, that context occurs, and meaning is added to words that in another context would have different or no meaning.

Neuroscientist Daniel Levitin reports "that ten thousand hours of practice is required to achieve a level of mastery . . . in anything."[2] Specific brain changes result from repetitive learning. The process for change varies depending on the nature of the stimuli. And there are immediate, intermediate and long-term processes. Stimuli may be subliminal and unconscious, but they initiate neural activity in one or more "brain switchboard" connections.

Chapter twenty-eight of the book of Isaiah gives us a beautiful illustration. When the people of Israel would not hear the word of the Lord, we are shown one of God's methods. Isaiah said, "Whom will he teach knowledge, and to whom will he explain the message? . . . For it is precept upon precept, precept upon precept, line upon line, line upon line, here a little, there a little" (vv. 9-10). Notice that even in describing the process for repetition, repetition is modeled. Over and over in the story of the Israelites, repetition is the technique described for leading the people into understanding. The brain responds to repetition.

Understanding the intricacies of neurobiology isn't necessary, but gaining familiarity with how the brain functions is important to those who would change the way people think.

PREACHERS ARE SOUL-REPAIR TECHNICIANS

Looking at the preacher as a technician—a soul technician—helps us to understand the requirements of the profession. Preachers who know the basics of human knowledge understand attention span, make allowance for age differences within the congregation and choose precise phraseology and vocabulary. Often ministers don't carefully choose the specific "tool" for a given sermon, a specific audience or a unique occasion for which a specially prepared sermon is needed. Yet no repair technician would attempt to repair an appliance without the special tool and knowledge of the occasion. The preacher should be no less prepared than an appliance technician, who must

- know the product;
- know what the product is built to do;
- have a depth of knowledge of the product manual;
- understand the mechanism of action;
- be acquainted with the more common problems;
- know how to be certain the problem is fixed.

Corollaries to this analogy may be found in preaching. The "product" is the congregant listener; the function is holy living; the product manual is the Bible; the mechanism of action is the work of the Holy Spirit in soul, mind and body; the common problem is "being human"; and a changed lifestyle and daily living demonstrate that the problem has been fixed.

Understanding better how the brain works and how the brain catalogs information based on past learning helps when choosing illustrations, object lessons, environmental changes, and liturgical and musical aspects, as well as when formatting information for attention and retention. The preacher's toolbox is as full as the creative mind can imagine.

MEMORY IS PRIMARILY DETERMINED BY IMMEDIATE NEED

Unless future necessities are made to have importance at the moment, memory of new information is stored for a future time and therefore has little immediate value—*unless* the future need is made clear. Maturity plays a major part in this process. The younger the child, the less he or she understands that what is learned today will be needed tomorrow. Similarly, many elderly people fail to accept new information, believing that they are so old that they will not need it in the future. Both are erroneous positions. This may be why adolescence and young adulthood are the optimal times for the integration of new knowledge, particularly sermons that present real-life lessons. For example, a college student may have little if any interest in a classroom lecture, but the immediate need is to learn information for an upcoming exam that will determine a course grade. Since sermon information is for today, tomorrow and beyond, learning how to make the sermon message an immediate need is mandatory.

BRAIN GATES ARE VALUABLE

Teachers in earlier times understood that effective teaching requires as much sensory input as possible. The senses can be thought of as gates into the brain. The understanding is simple: the more sensory modalities are engaged in preaching, the more likely it is that the brain will remember. When we *hear, see, feel, taste and smell*, all five sensory inputs into the brain are engaged. When we only hear, only one-fifth of the potential learning power is utilized.

Famous educational experiments were conducted in schools in Switzerland and northern Italy in the late 1800s and early 1900s that empirically proved the value of multisensory input. These schools were known as "sense-realism" schools.[3] If children could *see* a goat, *touch* the goat, *smell* the goat, *hear* the goat and *taste* the milk of the goat, they were not prone to forget the goat. Great teachers of that day, such as Pestalozzi, Froebel and Montessori, demonstrated pragmatically what has now been proven to be correct neuroscientifically: teaching for retention requires utilizing as many brain gates as possible.[4] According to Ray Jackendoff, "When a lexical item establishes a phonological connection to working memory, this also activates its syntactic and conceptual structures as well."[5]

For instance, the olfactory system (sense of smell) plays a significant role in learning, emotions and memory. It's the first of the twelve cranial nerves in the brain and is the most primitive of body senses. The olfactory nerve has direct connections to the limbic and paralimbic areas of the brain, which help us to learn and remember. Churches that utilize incense are using this "brain gate" to advantage. The odor is embedded in the brain and reminds the worshiper of what has been designated as sacred. Whether it's incense, burning food on the stove, smoke from a wood-burning fireplace or the pungent odor of burning rubbish, memory is elicited and a connection made. The stimuli may be new, but the memory that reifies it is not.

The early sense-realism school of thought and its methods are still used today, such as in Montessori schools and in most Sunday schools, though the teachers may not know it. For instance, the use of flannel boards, drama, costumes, object lessons and other sensory stimuli open more brain gates. Experiential learning, frequently out of necessity, includes this educational philosophy. However, methods that have proven to work with children are often ignored when teaching adults, even though humans learn by the same processes from cradle to grave.

Many adults love to listen to sermons addressed to children.

Adults enjoy watching the children, and they are instructed by sermons given in children's language accompanied with an object lesson. The mind (in both adults and children) continues to identify with objects to form associations and therefore memory. The *New York Times* reported that children as young as kindergarten age learn more quickly that a slice of pizza is such by seeing, touching, tasting, smelling one and hearing the word *pizza* than by simply being told the information.[6]

Here we introduce an important concept for connecting the brain to religion. Object lessons work, whereas words often have insufficient data to "tie back to" (*religare*). When we can't tie new information to old, it is often lost. Many scholars relate religion to its derivation from a reduplicated *religare*, . . . traced to Cicero . . . which required *going over again*. . . . Campbell insisted on theology being *ligare*, i.e., *to bind or reconnect* . . . which was adopted by St. Augustine. Many theologians and religion philosophers relate the combination of religion with *ligare* due to its historicity with Talmudic law. Hence, *religio* and *ligare* came to be associated with each other, particularly within religious education.

Rahner states, "An etymological study of the word *religion* will lead us to the notions of reconnecting and 'binding oneself back to one's origin and goal.'"[7] The English word *religion* is considered an extrapolation of *religare* according to Campbell and later by St. Augustine.[8] Therefore, if we are to hope for mature religious thinking, we must build the foundation to "tie back to." How adults think about God is directly related to the roots that have been nurtured in them as children, so that there is a basis for new thoughts to tie back to what is already accepted thinking. All thoughts must be objectified to become cognitive food for decision making and behavioral action. More will be said about this later when we discuss symbols and ritual.

A SCRIPTURAL ILLUSTRATION OF EARLY LEARNING

The book of Deuteronomy, which is the farewell sermon of Moses, illustrates this point very well. The children of Israel were instructed:

> Hear, O Israel: The LORD our God is one LORD: And thou shalt love the LORD thy God with all thine heart, and with all thy soul, and with all thy might. And these words, which I command thee this day, shall be in thine heart: And thou shalt teach them diligently unto thy children, and shalt talk of them when thou sittest in thine house, and when thou walkest by the way, and when thou liest down, and when thou risest up. And thou shalt bind them for a sign upon thine hand, and they shall be as frontlets between thine eyes. And thou shalt write them upon the posts of thy house, and on thy gates. (Deut 6:4-9 KJV)

It seems that Moses was convinced that the children of Israel could not learn by simple instruction. God's ways and commands were to be repeated throughout the day in various scenarios. As repetitious as it seems, and in truth was, they were to be reminded when walking, when going to bed and when awakening, and they were to write it on the doorposts and on the gates. The words were to be ingrained on their minds in every conceivable way, so they would have no excuse for not remembering them.

Jewish leaders in Old Testament times also wore phylacteries in the middle of their foreheads—"as frontlets between thine eyes." "The phylactery had four small compartments in which the following four passages of scripture were concealed: Exodus 13:1-10, 11-16; Deut. 6:4-9; 11:13-21."[9] Israel was constantly reminded of the law in multiple ways and mostly by repetition. Why repetition in so many different methods? Wasn't verbal instruction sufficient? No, it wasn't. The basis of neural learning may not have been known, but the pragmatics of the practice of repetition in as many ways as possible surely was.

Why was the repetition important? "When your children ask you in time to come, 'What is the meaning of the decrees and the statutes and the ordinances that the Lord our God has commanded you?' then you shall say to your children . . ." (Deut 6:20-21). The take-home lesson here is that we are to teach what children do not clearly understand at the time but with maturity will understand later.

This is an interesting illustration in that it recognizes the difference between what we tell children (due to their ability to understand it) and what we tell adults (due to what they have learned that can be built on). In this case, the premise is laid: Love the Lord completely; have no doubts about the love relationship. Then build on that premise: the child who asks later will be able to accept the hardships and promises of God. The foundation was laid for *religare*—that is, there was something poured in concrete to be tied back to.

According to Louis Cozolino, multiple neural networks are called into play when children and adults hear stories, including Bible stories. We connect the stories with objects and are encouraged to enter the plot of the story. The brain "maximizes the integration of a wide variety of neural networks. Through stories, we connect with others, share the words, thoughts, and feelings of the characters, and provide the opportunity for moral lessons, catharsis, and self-reflection."[10] Ernest Rossi states, "Although stories may appear imprecise and unscientific, they serve as powerful tools for the work of neural network integration at a high level."[11] Based on past experiences, children and adults inevitably, consciously or unconsciously, identify with a given character, plot and outcome.

LANGUAGE IS LEARNED IN RELATIONSHIP TO MEANING

Children learn language (including theological language) in *relationship to meaning, not meaning in relationship to language*. There is a solemn but valuable lesson in this for those who teach children, whether it is theology or something else. A child must first have a repertoire of words that are grounded in meaning.

We speak of *recognition*. The prefix *re* means "again," so this word presumes that the present cognition is connected to (*religare*) previous cognition. To recognize is to remember, reapply and otherwise revisit previous information. Ministers often preach as if their theological language is common to the layperson and that the theological-philosophical interpretations that come as second nature to the preacher are already well ensconced in the minds of the listeners. Not so. The minister would do well to employ symbols, object lessons, ritual and liturgy to make scriptural abstractions more concrete in both the biblically and the nonbiblically conversant mind. The brain can't *re*member unless it has other "members" to attach to—that is, previously accepted information.

Use as Much Brain Circuitry as Possible

Increasing the number of gates opened into the brain allows for a much higher likelihood that information will stick. There is now more than ample proof, according to Norman Doidge, that "neurons that fire together wire together."[12] We are now able to do brain mapping whereby we can see and map in hard copy what the brain is doing in a variety of differing situations. Brain maps show that we develop very strong highways that form major intersections when multiple neurons are activated simultaneously. The more neurons we can help to fire together, the more likely we are to develop those major intersections of learning, memory and decision making.

There is emerging evidence that although we still do not know exactly how the brain works, we know more and more about the neurochemical and neuroanatomical aspects of its operation. In a series of recent imaging studies, scientists discovered that a very thin slice of the parietal cortex (on the surface of the brain about an inch above the ears) is particularly active when the brain judges quantity. There are particular parts of human anatomy that seem adept at understanding quantity, and there is similar brain anatomy for understanding the concept of arranging and rearranging both old and new information into clusters that the brain then categorizes as memory patterns, behavioral cues and decision-making devices. Doidge has shown through repeated clinical and laboratory experiments that multiple parts of the brain are involved in nearly every human experience, and that some areas of the brain respond to extremely tiny bits of stimuli. His work and the resulting findings are far too complicated, and unnecessary for our discussion. However, it is helpful to appreciate the complexity and precision of the brain in sorting out the multiple layers of information being perceived by the brain every moment of the day, both while waking and when asleep.[13]

Researchers rightly suggest that the eyes are like cameras; they do not just see but also actually take pictures that are stored in the brain. With closed eyes, a person can see billions of images that are no longer within physical eyesight. For instance, the brain can see itself inside a cathedral with the sun flowing through the stained-glass windows, the old and well-worn oak pews with the faded, red velvet cushions, the hymnal in the rack and even the offering envelopes and a pencil in its holder. These visual memories aren't stand-alone mental processes. The image has an accompanying idea about what it all means and even accompanying decisions regarding those images. For one person it might mean lighting a candle, kneeling and praying; for another it might mean pagan worship.

BRAIN PHOTOGRAPHS ARE IMPORTANT

The important message, therefore, is that *the brain stores visual photographs for future use.* There may be a message here for churches that have no stained-glass windows, no architectural symbols, no outward signs of being a place of worship. Their images present photographic imprints on the brain that are very different.

Churches as well as preachers would do well to consider how

many potential gates to the brain they are utilizing. In forsaking symbolism such as stained-glass windows, the pulpit, the large open Bible and other visual reminders (memory enhancers), much learning potential is lost. It may well be that the Greek Orthodox Church, the Roman Catholic Church, the Anglican Church and lesser known communions with icons, incense, the taste of the Eucharist, colorfully vested clergy and other elements of tradition have a better chance of imparting information through more brain gates than churches that have no pulpit (the symbol of the sermon), no stained-glass windows to see, no hymnbooks to feel, no incense to smell, no large, open Bible and no vested clergy.

Symbols carry meaning. Whether it's a wedding ring, a church steeple or a traffic light, they all project a distinct message that evokes a specific thought and/or action. Churches that have largely eliminated traditional symbols have elected to forsake many powerful messages. Some people consider such symbols unnecessary— so much so that in some megachurches, there is no indication that it is a church. The auditorium has no religious symbolism. Therefore, what is the message? Has this church eliminated symbols? No, of course not; it has simply substituted the symbol of secularism or nonreligious symbols for the traditional stained-glass windows, icons and other "churchy" accoutrements. The commercial and industrial worlds have learned well how to use every gate possible for marketing temporary pleasures. Why should the church be less wise with its powerful symbols and resources?

VOCABULARY IS THE CURRENCY OF LEARNING

The vocabulary of the listener determines whether the sermon will be accepted or rejected. An immediate response is required and always given. However, since many times the language of the sermon is foreign to the listener, it is like a package being refused because the recipient can't understand the delivery person.

Language determines if the message is simply *delivered* by the speaker or *heard* by the listener. Starting in early childhood, we develop a vocabulary that is attached to meaning—usually objects, persons and activities. Our earliest infantile mumblings, only understood by ourselves, are tied to specific and absolute persons, objects and needs. Our lexicon, or individual dictionary, determines the meaning of a word or phrase. Through the years of growing, experiencing and learning, our lexicon morphs into greater meaning, with more complex and/or different responses to words we hear. Continuous and consistent teaching allows the development of deeply embedded belief systems based on both philosophical and pragmatic belief systems, which are, in the final analysis, language.

We all have our own private dictionary and its partner thesaurus. A single word has multiple meanings, and the meaning assigned to it by a listener is often entirely different from the meaning assigned to it by the speaker. The personal dictionary that each of us uses is more like an encyclopedia than a dictionary in that any given word represents a much larger picture than the narrow definition of a single word, even when that word is used in its appropriate context. "A lexical item is a complex association of phonological, syntactic, and semantic structures . . . *structures,* not just *features.*"[14]

So, preaching must be based on commonly understood words and contexts. All words by themselves offer such a wide variety of interpretations (according to our highly individualized dictionaries) that only with *repetitive varying explanations* can sermons be understood sufficiently for decision making. In this regard, we can understand Moses' instructions to teach God's ways in a wide variety of scenarios.

Theology assumes a commonly agreed-on lexicon for major belief systems. Preachers usually know this lexicon, and most parishioners know part of it. Huston Smith, an internationally renowned authority on religion, asserts that while individual differences may appear, value assumptions of the virtuous life tend to be nearly universal, even in the face of different religious beliefs.[15] Although such universalism is to a large degree true, the application of the beliefs and virtues varies significantly.

To be practical and prudent, we must think of those who listen within the context of their perceived needs, their immediate desires and their current belief system. If we are accurate in understanding the perceived needs of our audience and the immediacy of their needs, and if we can relate to their belief system, we will have a chance of succeeding with powerful preaching.

This is no small task. When people come to church overburdened by excessively busy and stressful lifestyles, it's paramount to understand that their cognitive structure is inhibited by problems that await them when the service is over. They must make the neural switch from daily problem solving to thinking about eternal matters if they are to hear and listen.

The preacher's life is centered on the theological premises of the profession. Although those in professions other than clergy and those in religious orders might adopt theological premises around which to work, that is seldom the case. The problem is that the preacher doesn't sufficiently take into account the very different world in which congregants live and work. They do not spend their days praying with the sick, performing weddings and funerals, and constantly immersing themselves in reading material related to next week's sermon. More time must be given by the preacher in figuring out ways to capture the folks in that other world and transport them into the worship world of preaching, so that they are at least in a similar frame of mind to enter into the preacher's world.

The preacher has presumably been mulling over the sermon material and living with those ideas all week. Reality sets in when the preacher realizes that the sermon is being given to a sea of relatively faithful, moderately interested but only marginally attentive people who need the service to get over with so they can get on with solving what they perceive as the real problems of daily life.

TECHNOLOGY DOES NOT REPLACE PREACHING

While today is a day of macro- and microtechnology and while many local congregations have adopted this rapidly evolving technology, there is no technology that replaces the spoken word: "How, then, can they call on the one they have not believed in? And how can they believe in the one of whom they have not heard? And how can they hear without someone preaching to them?" (Rom 10:14 NIV). Long before the dawn of modern technology, the brain assimilated and grew and made decisions based on the spoken word—and it still does today.

In the New Testament, the Greek word *kerygma* is translated "preaching," meaning "proclaiming," "announcing." It is related to *kēryx*, meaning "herald," and to *kēryssō*, which means "to announce, make known."[16] However, preaching is not simply talking in a different tone of voice, nor is it always words spoken by a minister in a church. Instead, it is the embodiment of the redemptive message in the person doing the preaching. Without question, it is *incarnation*—that is, "a living being embodying a deity or spirit."[17] The apostle Paul spoke of "Christ *in* you, the hope of glory" (Col 1:27, emphasis added).

The idea of "Christ-embodiment" is not alien to Protestant theology. It is said that Luther proclaimed that Christians acting as disciples are "little Christs." C. S. Lewis discusses the same concept: "Because of what the one true Son has done, the Father looks at us 'as if' we are a 'little Christ.'"[18] Thomas à Kempis (1380–1471) wrote an entire book on the "imitation of Christ," which is still considered a theologically sound Christian classic. If all followers are enjoined to be "little Christs," does this not implore the preacher to lead the flock accordingly?

Current knowledge of neuroscience assures us that the mind does change, and all things become new when the brain is transfixed by the power of the gospel. An actual anatomical, neural networking— the mechanism for thinking changes—results in conversion. Paul's otherwise somewhat elusive proclamation "If anyone is in Christ, he is a new creation" (2 Cor 5:17 NIV), remains a mystery but is no longer to be doubted. Evidences of postconversion experiences as well as emerging neurocognitive studies show that a mind transfixed undergoes change. Andrew Newberg writes,

> Once we believe that our perceptions accurately represent something in reality, the brain begins to send this information through a hierarchical processing system that allows us to compare the representation with our memories and other beliefs. These cognitive functions which are largely preconscious are the real magicians of the brain.[19]

Although Newberg attributes this to the plasticity of the neural pathways in the brain and although he is undoubtedly correct, the explanation discusses only the *mechanism* of change. The Scriptures discuss the *why:* because of faith.

3

The Brain Sees Preaching
as Unique

The power of the Lord was present with him to heal.

LUKE THE PHYSICIAN (LK 5:17)

How are they to believe in one of whom they have never heard? And how are they to hear without someone to proclaim him?

THE APOSTLE PAUL (ROM 10:14)

In the entire world, there is nothing like preaching from the pulpit in a church. Preaching is unique to the church; it is found nowhere else. In the whole world, there is nothing comparable to a sermon. No other organization presents "truth" from a pulpit in the same fashion as the church. The human brain is conditioned from infancy to see what the minister says as unique and demanding of respect. Even if the message is not believed or is rejected, the minister is still, for the most part, respected as a person.

Talks are given and speeches made, but only in the church is the sermon at home. The sermon stands alone in its ability to sway listeners' minds. It stands alone as the pedestal from which listeners have come to expect "word from on high." Regardless of the cynicism about or criticism of preachers and pulpits, the sermon remains high and lofty, even to those who do not believe. Preaching is proclamation. Agree or disagree, people listen and react. It is the preaching of the Word by which the human race shall be saved, according to the Scriptures (Rom 10:14-17; 1 Cor 15:1-2; 1 Pet 1:23-25).

Preaching as a proclamation is different from preaching simply to fulfill requirements in a worship service. Further, there is something powerful about the eyes of both the preacher and the hearer who communicate with eye contact. Those who preach without sufficient eye contact risk losing a vital part of communication— the power of visual relationship. When someone speaks to an audience, individuals may choose to believe that it is simply general information and not directed toward them. But when the preacher makes eye-to-eye contact, there is no doubt about the directionality of the words, and there is no doubt about the dynamic energy that flows between individuals when looking into each other's eyes.

The sermon stands for far more than the sermon as such. It represents in word power the sacraments and the communal life of the congregation. The words of the sermon are transported to become the very Word, no longer simply verbalizations, but de facto statements from God. It seems almost like blasphemy to think that a person actually interprets God to others, but it is so. Professor Richard Lischer of Duke Divinity School says, "Preaching is not a virtuoso performance but the language of the church that accompanies the laborious formation of a new people."[1]

In much church architecture, the pulpit was often higher than any other part of the sanctuary. It was not only high and lofty, but also ornate with hand-carved wooden, brass or gold symbols of the faith embedded in it. The choir and the congregation were forced to look up to the pulpit. It was not a matter of looking up to the preacher as a *person*, but as a representative of God; the purpose was to give proper ascendancy and elevated prominence to the preaching of the Word.

The pulpit positioned above the other parts of the sanctuary is still a powerful symbol. It may be likened to those congregations who see the open Bible as being central and therefore placed in the middle of the chancel, on the Communion table or in front of the pulpit. When speaking to the Israelites, Ezra held the Word high so everyone could see it, and he himself stood on a platform above the people (Neh 8:1-5). It's proper for the Bible to be held high as it is proclaimed to be the word of God.

The pulpit is the symbol and the resting place of the verbalized proclamation of that on which the church is built, by which it is sustained and for which it has its singular purpose. A current trend in some churches is for the minister to take a central place on the steps in front of the chancel or even to walk among the worshipers. This approach may have dramatic effect, but it is the pulpit and its message that is to be elevated, not the person verbalizing the Word.

It's most interesting that preaching has held a revered position in the church—as has public oratory in political and educational circles—but the church has not understood the scientific dynamics as to why it has always proven effective. However, we now live in a curious age when we not only ask why but also are given many answers through scientific research.

Knowledge from the neurosciences now validates the power of purposeful preaching. The spoken word proceeds through the hearing gate, and at that point it is just that—hearing. But the brain is capable of dealing with hearing in a variety of ways.

Hearing does not always result in listening. Swiss psychologist Jean Piaget (1896–1980), although he did not refer to preaching as such, helps us to understand how preaching actually works. Although some of his thinking and research has been called into question, many of his premises are still helpful to us and have been validated by modern neuroscience. After about age twelve, the brain becomes capable of thinking in hypothetical ways, is better able to convert what is heard into what is known, and subsequently integrates it into the pool of the "already believed." Abstract symbolic reasoning allows the human to translate by assimilating information from the environment into preexisting cognitive structures.

Beginning in infancy, the brain utilizes a process that Piaget called *assimilation* and another called *accommodation*.

> Assimilation occurs when something new is taken into the child's mental picture of the world, as when he acquires a younger brother or sister. Accommodation involves altering or reorganizing the mental picture to make room for a new experience or idea, as when the child must adjust his behavior to suit the enlarged family.[2]

That allows for change in the cognitive structure and thus in the ability to make decisions based on assimilation and accommodation. Assimilation must fit previously engrammed (stored) material,[3] and accommodation must fit the brain's need for functionality—that is, it must fit both thinking and behavior.

Piaget also demonstrated "that perceiving and reasoning unfold in development in the same way for all human beings, and that these processes are universal."[4] Although culture, language, environment and many other influences come to bear on intellectual development, in the final analysis, we all utilize these unique factors to *teach the brain* in similar ways.

This is where preaching comes in. Hearing and listening from birth until around age twelve equip the brain with millions of cognitive frameworks that change often and unpredictably. During those years, the human brain chooses its *methods* of cognition. These choices are made based on assimilation and accommodation, not based on adult decision making. By age seven, most children have internalized the cognitive processes that will serve as brain habits until around age twelve, when cognitive decision making is formalized.

The thinking of yesteryear (and often currently) was that children's thinking was mostly characterized by what the child's mind could *not* do. It was characterized in terms of "incapacity for abstract thinking, concept formation, connected judgment, and deduction."[5] Piaget emphasized the positive aspects of the child's mind: what the child is and what a child's mind can do.

Preachers *assume* that listeners understand what they are preaching. In fact, most parishioners can barely tell anyone what the sermon was about immediately after it is finished. I have repeatedly asked worshipers and found this unfortunate fact to be true. We would do well to revisit Nehemiah 8:

> All the people gathered together into the square before the Water Gate. They told the scribe Ezra to bring the book of the law of Moses, which the Lord had given to Israel. . . . And the ears of all the people were attentive to the book of the law. . . . And Ezra opened the book in the sight of all the people, for he was standing above all the people; and when he opened it, all the people stood up. Then Ezra blessed the Lord, the great God, and all the people answered, "Amen, Amen," lifting up their hands. Then they bowed their heads and worshiped the Lord with their faces to the ground. Also Jeshua, Bani, Sherebiah, Jamin, Akkub, Shabbethai, Hodiah, Maaseiah, Kelita, Azariah, Jozabad, Hanan, Pelaiah, the Levites, helped the people to understand the law, while the people remained in their places. So they read from the book, from the law of God, with interpretation. They gave the sense, so that the people understood the reading. (Neh 8:1, 3, 5-8)

The people then went their way with "great rejoicing, because they had understood the words that were declared to them" (Neh 8:12). The key word here is *understood.*

Understanding is the predecessor to decision. The brain can't change its thought process without understanding at some level—actually at several levels, although sometimes the level is purely physical, anatomical or even chemical in nature. Decisions can be made only after understanding.

Much thinking and programming that restricts the exposure of a child to theological concepts is based on faulty pre-Piaget thinking. Piaget insisted—and now we know that he was correct—that children's brains are malleable and impressionable. The process now known as "neuroplasticity"—that is, the ability of the brain to change itself—was not known in Piaget's time, but he demonstrated it in action. The transitional childhood mind allows for a *time* and *form of thinking* that can be harnessed for deeply engrammed memories. The impressionability and learning capacity of this stage in life must not be ignored. Ministers who do not capitalize on this rich period of life lose that unique gate into the soul forever.

Modern neuroscience recognizes this process as one of the factors in neuroplasticity—that is, the fluidity rather than the static nature of the brain. *Neuroplastic* refers to the brain's ability to reorganize itself by forming new neural connections throughout life. The precise definition of neuroplasticity is "a concept that neurons are not necessarily fixed in their functioning but are capable of functional modification as a result of changes of environmental signals."[6] Throughout life, the brain develops new circuits and neural connections both for growth and for repair. These connections are the "light switches" that turn on and off all thoughts and actions. The common understanding is that children's minds are moldable. While this is true, the concept of molding assumes outside pressure that forces material into a preconceived shape. This is an incorrect model for talking about the development of a child's brain. A better model is that from *within* a child develops judgment, intelligence and abstract thinking and deduces according to prelearned concepts the best method for self-preservation, gratification and growth.

Some teachers (and preachers) act as if the theory of tabula rasa, a theory promulgated by John Locke (1632–1704), is correct—that is, children are born with a "blank slate" and can be indoctrinated without preconceived knowledge. He believed that knowledge comes only from postnatal experience, which is now known to be utterly false. We build on what is there, from the earliest stages of gestation. This may be considered "primordial learning," in that it is neurochemical, neuroanatomical and noncognitive.

Andrew Newberg, a noted neuroscientist, wrote, "As far as we can tell, newborns have no discernible beliefs, because the newborn brain is at a primitive stage of development, barely able to integrate sensory information."[7] We also know without question that the underpinnings of infant learning are clearly present in the latter stages of gestation and that the fetus responds to sounds as well as environmental stimuli.

> Inside the womb, surrounded by amniotic fluid, the fetus hears sounds. It hears the heartbeat of its mother, at times speeding up, at other times slowing down. And the fetus hears music . . . the auditory system is fully functional about twenty weeks after conception.[8]

With better understanding of the stages at which information is accepted and stored, preachers are more able to speak so that others can listen. Since most preachers have a mix of people in the congregation, careful thought about sentence structure, the illustrations used, the logical sequence of the sermon contents and the method of sermon delivery is necessary. Although much of "gestational learning" is still not understood, fewer doubts about it survive each year. No one assumes it to be cognitive "thinking" per se, but few if any have doubts about the neurological, neurochemical and neuroplastic abilities of the brain to lay the foundations during pregnancy for developing thought processes.

References to prenatal experiences can be found in many ancient texts, from Hippocrates's journals to the Bible. "The realization that even the rudiments of language may be laid down in the womb has taken full circle. Forty years ago, such a notion would have been dismissed as impossible, while four hundred years ago, it would have been accepted as a matter of fact."[9] Now, twenty-five years later, modern science no longer doubts this knowledge and respects the fact that over a thousand years ago, the Chinese established prenatal clinics to guide expectant mothers through their pregnancies both emotionally and physically.

As well as misunderstanding learning processes, preachers frequently assume that those hearing have a similar religious upbringing and assume that they operate from the same vocabulary and definitions of words. Such assumptions leave many minds out in the cold, since parochial vocabulary is truly foreign to less theologically trained minds, to say nothing of many denominational, ethnic and geocultural factors. For them, entering into the preacher's vocabulary and definitions is as strange as it would be for the average minister to enter into the middle of an advanced neurospectrophotometric lecture. The difference is that both the parishioner and the minister *assume* a common meaning and do not admit the incredible discrepancy between the two.

Knowledge of the various human developmental stages indicates at which age each kind of preaching is most apt to achieve results. Sunday school and children's worship make sense. Children ask *what*, and adolescents ask *why*. Newberg stated,

> Neurophysiologically, adolescence corresponds to a time in which the overall metabolism in the brain begins to decrease. Neural pruning continues (and will continue until metabolic stability is reached at around thirty). Cognitive processes become stabilized, and the remaining neural connection will govern our thinking and behavior for the rest of our lives (taking into account changes due to neuroplasticity). During adolescence, a person's basic beliefs about life, relationships,

and spirituality gradually mesh into a coherent worldview, but adolescents continue to struggle between conformity and independence.[10]

There have been several attempts to build a model for what might be called "spiritual development." Probably the most famous is that of James Fowler of Candler School of Theology. All developmental models are intrinsically psychological in nature, having been conceptualized largely from Erik Erikson's (1902–1994) psychological developmental model, assuming some "sameness" between psychological and spiritual. For the purposes of this book, it's simpler to consider spiritual development as just that: conceptualized as spiritual rather than in the larger context of psychology. Therefore, such a consideration might look more like the following:

- Stage one: Belief (from birth, the infant places primitive trust in the mother for food, warmth, safety and preservation needs)

- Stage two: Spiritual self (early childhood becomes a self-centered place; belief that environment will be self-serving)

- Stage three: Self-affirming faith (validates the self; that which is believed is found to be mostly true, at least "believed" to be true)

- Stage four: Positive, productive faith (enables one to become productive within growing doubts but mostly shared beliefs)

- Stage five: Established personal belief (ambiguity lessens; faith serves to stabilize life)

- Stage six: Interpersonally shared belief system (builds relationships around common belief-based goals)

- Stage seven: Contributory belief system (gives back to relationships, organizations, community, etc.)

- Stage eight: Confident internalized hope (tranquil amid life changes, not fearful of death)[11]

While most developmental models attempt to correlate "faith" stages with chronological ages, it isn't possible to be accurate, since a person may be chronologically an adult but a "babe in the faith," or conversely, may be only a teenager but quite mature in faith. Further, stages of faith are not necessarily stable; a person may move between (regressive as well as progressive) faith stages, regardless of chronological age.

Children in religious instruction classes are taught the "what," and churches are given the opportunity to follow through with adolescents in answering the "why." The church often loses its adolescents when cognitive decision making is most important, thus potentially losing them for life.

To understand how our preaching becomes acceptable information to the brain, we must consider the process of *engramming*, that is, how the brain accepts and stores information and makes it permanent. Although he did not coin the word *engram*, Piaget presented us with that concept, which has been more than substantially proven by neuroscientists. An engram is a hypothetical pathway in the brain created by new experiences and information. These pathways become "memory traces" on which all information that follows is built. Engrams provide a pathway over which impulses can travel easier than attempting to assimilate and accommodate new information that does not fit these pathways. Impulses may be chemical or electrical stimuli which reactivate "old learning," yet at other times initiate new learning; hence, the accumulation of new information. The human brain is uniquely equipped to differentiate such signals.

Here we begin to understand why early learning is so important in making later decisions. We understand how preaching and teaching establishes engrams early in life that form the understanding and acceptance of theological constructs in later childhood. We now know why such learning becomes not only easier but also more automatic after the cognitive decision-making stage at around age twelve.

To understand engramming better, we can think of imprinting or branding. However, these analogies are not entirely accurate; as a matter of fact, they are contrary. Imprinting and branding are forces from the outside that place information *on* not *in.* Cattle with a brand have a mark *on* the skin, not *in* the animal. Embossing or imprinting places information *on* but not *in* the paper or leather. The process of outside to inside is different from the process of inside to outside. Much teaching and education is from outside to inside, and therefore of little value. The gospel, by definition, is from inside to outside. Being able to plant something inside that can permanently and indelibly function from the inside out is exactly what preaching is about. The watermark woven into a piece of stationary is a more accurate analogy, in that the embedded identification is an inseparable part of the whole.

Webster's Encyclopedic Unabridged Dictionary defines *engram* as "a durable mark caused by a stimulus upon protoplasm."[12] Preaching *does* indeed attempt to produce a "durable mark" in the thinking brain. This is where engramming helps us to understand preaching. What is heard is then listened to by the brain and followed by finding acceptable engrammed pathways that have already been prepared to assimilate and accommodate new information.

Engramming is a usable concept in spiritual as well as intellectual development. In fact, the forces for spiritual "enlightenment" are so omnipresent that engramming occurs both with and without our knowledge and intent. Moving through the various stages of spiritual development calls on different styles and methods for engramming at different times and in different circumstances. The church and the sermons (all teachings) of the church must recognize the various needs of each unique person, the person's age, the environment and the circumstance, and adapt methodology accordingly.

So, all of this helps us to understand what we already know but do not always practice—namely, that preaching is indeed unique. It provides building blocks from early childhood onward and actually prepares the brain to make adult decisions, which when addressed continuously and sequentially make for easy, if not almost automatic, adult decisions.

4.

The Brain Uses Preaching
for Healing

The human brain is constantly looking for integration, synthesis, pleasure and hope. Nothing offers these possibilities more unconditionally than preaching. When speaking of healing, most think of body healing and then possibly mind, but healing is much more inclusive than mind and body. The mind is healed, and relationships and communities are healed, while emotional pain and despair are replaced with hope and peace. There is scientific evidence to prove this. Faith, which is the basis for spiritual healing, is enhanced with brain-based preaching.

The brain is accustomed to looking for hope. Hope and healing are inseparable; where there is hope, there is healing, and where there is healing, there is hope. Hope offers healing for the here and now and continued healing for the future. In actuality, hope is pure faith—and so it is the basis of all healing.

The basic premise of the entire Bible is healing—that is, wholeness, completeness, the reunification of creation with Creator. Sometimes it's called reconciliation, and sometimes it is called salvation, but in all instances, the basic biblical demand and the invitation of God is for *healing*—personal, interpersonal and beyond.

When Jesus came preaching and teaching, he also performed healings that demonstrated the compassion of God and, more importantly, authenticated Jesus' atoning mission as Messiah. The Gospel of Matthew states, "That evening they brought to him many who were possessed with demons; and he cast out the spirits with a word, and cured all who were sick. This was to fulfill what had been spoken through the prophet Isaiah, 'He took our infirmities and bore our diseases'" (Mt 8:16-17; see also Is 53). Jesus told John's disciples that his healings prove that he is the Messiah (Mt 11:2-6). His ultimate mission was to satisfy God's wrath against sin. He accomplished this on the cross and reconciled us to God, healing the ancient breach between Creator and creation caused by sin (Gal 3:13; 2 Cor 5:18-21). Jesus' atoning work on the cross, the new life we are given through faith and the healing we are given through faithfulness is the gospel message that must be preached to the world.

If preaching this essential message does not command attention, it is overrun in the parishioner's mind by a myriad of other tapes and recorded messages both from years ago and from those encountered on the way to the church, for example. Preaching that is purposefully focused can, by the use of theologically sound and neuropsychologically proven methods, overcome this mind noise so that those who hear the gospel are healed.

The brain understands the difference between meditative activity and verbal stimuli. Both initiate neuronal activity and both have the ability to move the brain—that is, to change the way we think. So, both activities—meditative and acoustic—are important in worship. When verbal stimuli are presented first, they are followed by the meditative, which allows the verbal input to be massaged, classified and reorganized into thoughts. When meditation is first, the brain sorts out the internalized stimuli and processes it for personal decision making. We find both kinds of worship identified in the Scriptures. "Be still and know that I am God" is one kind (meditative). Paul preaching on Mars Hill is another (acoustic). Each works in tandem with the other, and neither is fully functional in the brain until both processes are engaged.

The brain determines what to do with what it experiences. Therefore, if healing is to result from what might be called religious stimuli, it must make sense to both the emotional needs of the psyche and the neuropsychological associations within the brain. The Scriptures are not always helpful in this process when they are isolated from real experiences. Without direct application, many hearers will listen to stories (including Bible stories) as being about other people at other times in other places with no application to themselves in the present.

Many view public preaching as education, lecturing, instruction, teaching and edification; and it is all of that, but infinitely more. At the very base, preaching is healing in the deepest and broadest sense of the word *healing*, for to heal is to make whole. Therefore, when discussing preaching, we must include the latest information on how the brain works.

Good preaching must be applied uniquely to the preacher before it can be made public, thus allowing the power of the sermon to heal the messenger first. The preacher first digests the message and, after finding the discourse instructive and healing, is able to apply it to others. If the preacher is not made more whole by the content, there is little hope that others will benefit from it either. After the preacher has faced the truths and convictions of the Word in the privacy of the study and personal prayer, it may then—and only then—be viewed as appropriate for congregational consumption.

Purposeful Preaching Is Worship

Both preaching and worship must be *purposeful* for healing. Worship need not be formal—within an organization or communal setting—but the *act of worship* is a necessary corollary of preaching and must be *intentional*—that is, specifically planned with specific goals in mind. Healing is always within a context; the context is inextricably interwoven with the Scriptures, the Scriptures with preaching and the preaching within the context of the gathered people. The Scriptures become the incarnate Word of God proclaimed by the chosen messenger. Therefore, preaching is not a *part* of worship. Preaching *is* worship.

The idea that preaching is simply one element among other worshipful aspects of a service places the Word in a role subordinate to what may be considered intimate or personal. Worship is communal and worship is individual. Preaching is both as well. The preached word contains the power of individual and group transformation. *Worship*, by definition, refers to the unique experience of relating our innermost selves to God, both in soliloquy and in concert. Preaching begins with the private, communal relationship of the preacher to the Creator of the preached Word. Only after this kind of intimacy can the preaching become an integral part of the worship—that is, the publicly proclaimed revelation that has come from the intensity of that most sacred moment when *God* has spoken and *the preacher* has listened.

Preaching as worship distinguishes between earthly holiness—or human holiness—and God's holiness. Human holiness is valued by nearly the entire human race. It includes trying to be kind, attempting to love enemies, trying to tell the truth, striving to have good motives and much more. These are all commendable goals. However, they are the demonstrations of human effort. We, as humans, are always trying, but only in God's perfection are we able to *do it* rather than to *try it*. This is the very core of worship—God's holiness.

A worshipful experience of preaching allows the folly of our efforts and the superior power of God's grace to be shown. Only those who worship "in spirit and truth" (Jn 4:24) see preaching as worship. In this passage, Jesus was talking with the Samaritan woman at the well—the woman with five husbands—and clearly pointing out to all of us that worship requires both *spirit* and *truth*;

the combination of spirit and truth is truly brain work. *Spirit works on the soul; truth works on the brain; and both are important attributes of the Holy Spirit.*

Often sermons attempt to tune listeners in to their own spirits and carefully avoid truth. They assume that relating and engaging the emotional aspects of the faith will promote true faith (or at least faithful attendance). Such assumptions are faulty, since the engagement is to a prejudicial fervor, not the spirit of "truth." We must carefully discern between "the wind [that] blows where it chooses" (Jn 3:8) and our own wind that blows our nonbiblical sails. This passage is no doubt speaking of the work of the Holy Spirit—the *power* of the Holy Spirit. The preacher can rightly be expected to provide the truth from years of study and meditation in the Scriptures. At other times, overzealous evangelists have been so caught up in what they perceive as truth that they forget the necessary ingredient of spirit (that is, the Holy Spirit) and act as if they were responsible *and able* to provide both.

The apostle John tells us that "the Father seeks such as these to worship him" (Jn 4:23). True worship comes from the combination of recognizing that we sit in God's presence (God is spirit) and hearing the truth. On this premise, Jesus proclaimed, "I am the way and the truth and the life" (Jn 14:6). In this awesome atmosphere, preaching for healing occurs.

The atmosphere in which the sermon is heard is critical also.

No speaker preaches a sermon apart from a medium of encounter, and that medium is the church. . . . Protestantism has a long history of flaunting the Word above the sacraments and liturgy, as if, in Barth's words, preaching were not an interpretation of the sacrament, having the same meaning "but in words."[1]

This proclamation of Lischer, quoting Barth from previous writings, is critical in understanding the role of the preacher in relation to other aspects of ministerial duties and simultaneously elevating the Word while not lessening the sacred importance of sacraments and liturgy and while recognizing that preaching is the embodiment of the sacramental message.[2]

Since this book is primarily for the minister, emphasis is placed on preaching rather than attendance, but attendance is a necessary component for hearing the Word. This is self-evident, but it does remind clergy to encourage attendance and to recognize that preaching occurs in context—the context of the communal body of believers assembled at regular intervals.

To identify with Christ, we are required to identify with the burdened, the downtrodden, the ill and afflicted, the poor and the prisoners. Worshipful preaching is then seen not simply as *preaching* but also as *proclaiming* the "day of the Lord" intentionally and identifying personally with the Man of Sorrows, from his ignoble birth through his crucifixion, death, burial and, most important, his resurrection. For "if Christ has not been raised, your faith is futile" (1 Cor 15:17).

To understand preaching as worship, we need to look carefully at the concept of worship in the Scriptures. In defining *worship*, we usually think of the dictionary definition, which is to give reverence and honor—"honor, dignity, reverence, devotion."[3] No one can deny the experience of worship when sitting in a beautiful cathedral or church with the stained-glass windows, organ music, icons and the accompanying ecclesiastical accoutrements. However, this is only *one* experience of worship, and although it can be communal, it is uniquely individual. This description best fits the dictionary definition. Translated into modern jargon, the definition of worship is being quiet, surrounded by soft music, whispering and acting pious. The biblical definition of worship is very different.

When talking to the woman at the well, Jesus debunked the earthly definition of worship. He made it clear that it is not *where* we worship, but *how* and *what* we worship. To be in worship, we must worship the One who is the message, the One whom we believe *incarnates* the preacher, the One who promotes the essential voice of God, which continues the worship in the brain long after the sermon has ended.

The Old Testament usage of the word *worship* is akin to many people's definition of quiet reverence, while the New Testament accepts this rendering as a base and builds on it. Both the Hebrew word *šāḥah* and the Greek word *proskyneō* imply the reverential attitude of bowing down. However, "the New Testament idea of worship is a combination of the reverential attitude of mind and body, the ceremonial and religious service of God."[4]

THE MEANING OF FAITH TO PREACHING

The undisputed basis for spiritual healing is faith. Healings documented in the New Testament are based on faith—mostly on the part of the one seeking the healing. Sometimes the faith wavers a bit, such as the faith of the father who brought his son with the "dumb spirit" (probably a seizure disorder) to Jesus. Jesus told him, "If you are able!—All things can be done for the one who believes" (Mk 9:23). After the man declared, "I believe; help my unbelief," Jesus healed his son.

We do not know how faith works. If we did, it would no longer be faith. However, there are many things we know about faith. We know that faith is not magic, but it is mystical. We know that faith can be exhibited and encouraged. We know that preaching based on the principles in this book can encourage and promote faith. We know that the lack of faith can be challenged by exhortation and biblical preaching. We know that faith can be modeled by the preacher and, as in any role modeling, promote faith in others. And we know that the results of faith can be celebrated.

We must also differentiate *faith* from *belief*. Belief (at least conscious belief) is an intellectual pursuit. Whether it emanates from the rational or irrational mind makes no difference; belief is belief—

factual or not, reality based or not. As an intellectual activity, belief is based on assumptions that are coherent to the mind—even a disordered mind. *Webster's New World College Dictionary* defines belief as "the state of believing; conviction or acceptance that certain things are true or real." It also gives a second definition as related to faith, especially religious faith.[5] Newer neuroscience sheds doubt on these definitions, since faith and belief, although related and inseparable, clearly are not the same. Webster's would tend to make faith and belief synonymous yet distinguishable from each other. We can't blame earlier definitions for this confusion, but now that we are assembling neuroscientific data regarding the specifics of brain function, we know there is a difference. Belief can be studied scientifically; faith can't be studied except by observed results.

Since most people, including academicians and clergy, also tend to use these words synonymously, it's important to emphasize the difference. Although our vocabulary often engages ambiguity, the brain does not; it is more like a computer, which registers whatever key is pushed, regardless of what was intended. The brain absorbs the already programmed meaning of a word and acts on that previous knowledge. Little wonder that when people are faced with the question "When did you first believe?" they confuse that with living the life of faith. The two experiences are not the same and most often do not occur simultaneously. The *Encyclopedia of Religion* helps us by rendering a much clearer definition: "Faith is the giving of oneself to be controlled and remade by what commands trust and devotion."[6]

The word *faith* occurs only twice in the Old Testament (Deut 32:20; Hab 2:4), but it is frequent in the New Testament. *Faith* often connotes the Sanskrit root "to bind" or "to unite" (*religare*). This is very helpful to preachers and indicates the need to "tie back" (*religare*) what is being preached to what has already become accepted truth. It allows the intellectual instilling process of belief to access the establishing process of faith. One might say that it allows us to have faith in what we believe.

The *Encyclopedia of Religion* also helps to understand the scope of faith: "Faith is the giving of oneself to be controlled and remade by what commands trust and devotion."[7] The perfect example of the difference between belief and faith is Jesus himself. At age twelve, Jesus conveyed his belief system to the astonishment of the teachers in the temple: "And all who heard him were amazed at his understanding and his answers" (Lk 2:47). And the human of humans lived and died via a life of faith, as seen in what he said in the hours before his crucifixion: "Abba, Father, for you all things are possible; remove this cup from me; yet, not what I want, but what you want" (Mk 14:36). Mark helps us to understand the difference between belief and faith by pointing us to the life of Jesus, who *believed* that God could do all things, but trusted (*faith*) in what God wanted.

BELIEF AFFECTS FAITH—FAITH AFFECTS BELIEF
The interrelationship of faith and belief can't be taken lightly. Negative (or positive) belief systems create neural pathways that lead to evolving emotional bases on which faith systems are built.

Sometimes religious belief is referred to as "blind faith." There is no such thing as blind faith. This common sarcasm assumes that faith in someone or something can't be proven. Yet that is precisely why it is *faith*. On the other hand, we must be careful to distinguish faith from magic, which is deception. "The language of faith invites us to ponder mystery," homiletics professor John Suk says.[8] He is absolutely right—and mystery is not magic but truth as yet unverified by scientific explanation.

This difference is not merely academic. It matters substantially in the discussion of spirituality, theology and preaching. The preacher has the dual task of *instilling belief* while *establishing faith*. Instilling belief is basically done by preaching, utilizing every available brain gate into the intellect and thought processes of the brain. Establishing faith is quite another matter. Such establishment comes only from seeing the results of the instilled belief. This is where the modeling and celebration of faith comes in.

Faith is not intellectually based. Most of us from early childhood know that belief and faith are not the same. We learn early that we must "believe" something—that is, practice that belief—although we have no faith that it will work. Until we know more about the possibility of faith having some anatomical or chemical basis, we must assume it to be emotionally based. But neuroscience is certain now that simply because something is emotionally based does not mean it is unreal. Andrew Newberg literally lives on the cutting edge of neuroscience and declares that we continue to discover the literal neural bases of emotion and belief systems which increasingly reveal the "how" as well as the "why" of our thinking.[9] Brains are susceptible to imitation. When instilled belief produces recognizable, faith-based results, the brains of followers are quick learners.

Information, emotion, faith and belief are relatives. Information and belief are siblings but not twins; faith and emotion also have similarities but are not the same thing. Preachers' beliefs become the information that they share with others through their lifestyle, lectures, sermons and even casual conversation. Belief becomes emotion as it directly affects the fervency with which listeners respond to information. Information may be seen as entering the brain as neurological stimuli (hearing, seeing, and so on), and then being neurochemically translated into emotion (that is, how you *feel* about what you just heard) and then into belief (accept as true or reject as false). Once this is accomplished, the new belief takes on its emotional uniform and, with the authority of that belief, proclaims it as truth. This is the cycle from *information in* to *information out* that we call learning.

5

The Core Process of Preaching
Is Brain Work

Preach the word; be instant in season, out of season;
reprove, rebuke, exhort with all longsuffering and doctrine.

PAUL (2 TIM 4:2 KJV)

Preaching allows the brain to rethink, reorganize, reconnect and reconstruct itself as it creates new neurological pathways; neuroscience has shown us how the brain literally retrains itself in new ways of thinking. Preaching offers the possibility for the brain to change itself—not just in thinking but in actual anatomy. Preaching with intentionality *challenges* the brain of the listener.

A sermon comes to a congregation in direct preaching and in the aspects of worship. For instance, the Roman Catholic Church places emphasis on a homily (short sermon) that leads up to the apex of the message of the Eucharist. Protestants do likewise, except the sermon tends to be longer than a homily, and the message of the Eucharist (that is, Christ's substitutionary atonement) is not celebrated by the cup and bread at every worship service. Both are "preaching" the same message. Attempting to get the message across is done in various ways in different denominations, but the end message is the same. The methodology is different but the intent to make the brain work toward belief and faith is identical. Preaching, in whatever form, is brain work.

The primary purpose of preaching is to get inside the parishioner's heads. Getting into another's brain is easy—and very difficult. To do so, there must be a promise of reward with minimal pain. Pain can stop the brain from intellectual work and revert it to self-protection.

We must recognize that pain includes much more than usually thought. The Scriptures remind us,

> We know that the whole creation has been groaning in labor pains until now; and not only the creation, but we ourselves, who have the first fruits of the Spirit, groan inwardly while we wait for adoption, the redemption of our bodies. For in hope we were saved. Now hope that is seen is not hope. For who hopes for what is seen? But if we hope for what we do not see, we wait for it with patience. (Rom 8:22-25)

The human brain searches for evidence for any ability to heal. It yearns for wholeness and thus is in constant search for ways to correct the broken relationships between God and human beings and among human beings, to heal the soul, mind and body of each of us. In recent years, more emphasis has been placed on the necessity to heal society.

Here we see the brain burning a great amount of energy, literally working hope against hope. The intellectual brain is thrown into conflict with the emotional brain (mind), and thus struggles to find homeostasis. Preaching adds to the confusion and *intentionally* engages this kind of mental/emotional conflict. In the conflict, Christians believe the Holy Spirit clarifies God's plan. It's here that the Scriptures elucidate the necessity to "be still, and know that I am God" (Ps 46:10). This intellectual/emotional firestorm forces the brain amid the wind, fire and rain to separate belief from faith. Hebrews, known as the "faith chapter" of the Bible, recounts story after story of patriarchs who met this struggle with mind-altering faith, and "all of these died in faith without having received the promises" (Heb 11:13).

This kind of brain work forces the body to go against societal "common sense," and seeks to nullify that which cannot be physically seen and experienced by our five senses. Preaching appeals to a higher level of reasoning that is not found in the description of brain and body as we know it. Faith represents a phenomenon only understood by those who possess it. When wrestling with new information, the brain tests it against the crucible of tradition, personal experience, "modern thinking" and peer acceptance. This process is literally a wrestling match and requires the expenditure of much mental energy as well as personal motivation.

This is tough brain work. All aspects of the worship service are intended to focus our thinking on the message of the day. The message is more than the sermon; preaching is more than the sermon. The sermon is found in the hymns, the prayers, the Scripture readings and the spoken word. Our thinking, emotions, cognitive structures and much that we do not yet know about are involved. The sermon is part of this process if it is central—if it is indeed the reification of the Scriptures for the problems of life.

The sermon must be given the prominence of Moses presenting the Ten Commandments, Jeremiah decrying the wickedness of the people, John the Baptist crying out in the wilderness, Jesus casting out the demons, Paul preaching to the masses and the apostle John proclaiming the powerful language and metaphor of the Revelation. They did not preach as if the information was elective; it is mandatory for the survival of souls, nations and civilizations. The sermon must contain things that we *must* hear. It must also convince us that we *need to hear* those things. Although Protestants call it the sermon and Roman Catholics call it the homily, the intent and import are the same.

The brain is engaged if the core message of the preaching is embodied in all aspects of the service. The core message is given in words, music or sacrament. The brain sorts out that core message—and it may not be what the preacher intended, unless done with *intentionality*. The brain will not—and indeed cannot—occupy itself with unessential information. As with all other physiological activity, the brain attempts to conserve energy. Only what is essential to the preservation and enhancement of the person is entertained, so the absolute core of all preaching must be to engage the thought processes that trigger the emotional underpinnings of personal reward. Much of preaching has centered on the emotions of punishment countered by the reward of heaven. The brain is far more receptive to accessing the reward to avoid punishment than it is to avoiding punishment to obtain the reward. In other words, we do not enjoy having to go around the bad to get to the good if we can go directly to the good.

Although preaching addresses the entire congregation, it must be personal. "The stove is dangerous" and "the stove will burn me" are very different concepts. One is a statement of fact; the other is a reflection from personal experience. The brain makes an object of the dangerous thing without necessarily relating it to anything personal. It is a dangerous object, not necessarily to be avoided. When the stove is seen as something that will burn *me*, the meaning changes dramatically. Sermons that do not apply to the lives of the worshipers are objectified—that is, put into the category of "useful information" but "not for me." When we are infants, we develop the wish for immediate and pleasant gratification, and although with maturity we learn to delay it, internally we still want it and strive for it. When a preacher gives a sermon with the authority it deserves, it is more apt to be understood subjectively and personally applied.

Many great preachers were masters at showing how living a holy life offers pleasure and prevents pain. Avoiding pain and enjoying pleasure is certainly a hook that is both biblical and neurobiologically sound. Being able to personalize the sermon is a skill that pays big dividends.

Of all people, preachers armed with Holy Writ should be able to persuade an otherwise distracted audience of the values of avoiding the stresses of sinful living that lead to illness of mind, body and soul. But this can be done only if the sermon is given the position, reality, authority, prominence and time allotment necessary to make it central in the worship service. The sermon must be central in liturgical sequence, central in prominence, central in ideation and central in the congregation's experience.

We live in a world where our senses are bombarded with information and marketing schemes. The cacophony of brainwashing is mind boggling and does not stop when we go to sleep or attempt to shift our focus to another subject. Whatever programs itself all day continues in the subconscious for many hours, or even days. How often have you heard an advertising jingle and just couldn't get it out of your head? It plays over and over. Powerful sermons can do the same thing.

The minds of people who attend church are still whirring at a mile a minute with information just received over the radio or off the billboards read on the way to the church, potentially blocking out new information. The crucial question is, "How does the minister redirect and capture the minds of those who are already immersed in a plethora of other information?"

One answer is found in the neurosciences. The mind responds to what is most urgent for survival, gratification and growth. Capitalizing on this fact, news media outlets have immersed their audiences in dramatic headlines that market anger, frustration and fear: "The end of the world is near." "Terrorism is an imminent danger." "We will have an economic meltdown." "Global warming will destroy our way of life." Within only a few years, topics that are hotly debated and often disputed have changed academic curricula, the economy and human behavior worldwide. People today often feel overwhelmed by forces out of their control. There seems to be wave after wave of global emergencies.

If the mind is overwhelmed by survival issues, it is not ready to be gratified with what is presented. A story is told of a salesman who returned to his home office without selling anything and told his boss that it wasn't his fault because "you can lead a horse to water, but you can't make it drink." To this the boss replied, "Yes, but your job is to make the horse thirsty." Often—maybe most of the time—the job of the minister is to stimulate thirst in the audience. They will then seek the water and enjoy being served by the water bearer.

What does this have to do with preaching? Parishioners must understand the immediate gratification of peace with God, the tools to live in harmony with each other and the long-term survival value of living by a code of conduct that deflects conflict, lessens stress, permits emotional tranquility in the midst of chaos and has implications for eternity.

Brain Work also Involves the Body

The brain does not function alone. Author Gustav Eckstein pointed out the specific relationship of the brain to each organ in the body, and he correctly titled his book *The Body Has a Head*. Paul, the writer of the book of Romans, beseeches us to "present your bodies as a living sacrifice" (Rom 12:1).

The body responds to instructions from the anatomical switchboard in the brain. Although healing involves the entire body with all its organs and systems, the brain controls the entire process. We no longer hold to a dichotomy of mind and body. Today's scientific world promulgates a holistic approach to the human. The mind acts on the body, and the body acts on the mind. The minister that preaches in a way that acknowledges this promotes the healing of both body and mind.

Every aspect of life presents unique needs for healing, such as those dysfunctions that we call illnesses. Much brain work utilized in dealing with body and mental dysfunction is so routine and commonplace that it goes unrecognized consciously. But these circumstances do require brain work for resolution and accommodation. Ordinary circumstances still produce conflict, disharmony and dysfunction. Even physical disease—that is, dis-ease—is the inability of the body to deal with the effects of viral, bacterial and traumatic chaos. Bruce Lipton, the author of *The Biology of Belief* (2005), presents an interesting metaphor he calls the "get set" phenomenon, correctly postulating that the stresses of life keep us literally on our toes and ready to pounce. This phenomenon keeps the immune system under constant strain, the brain hyperalert and the physiology of the body never at ease—always at dis-ease.

As humans, we all live in a state of worldwide dis-ease that threatens our peace continually. "Eastern Christianity offers a helpful understanding of dis-ease, it is called 'ancestral' sin . . . and the rest of the human race, as well as all of creation, inherit the results. . . . We have inherited a sick state of existence (dis-ease, dis-connection)."[1] The Old Testament also speaks of ancestral sin: "punishing the children for the sin of the fathers to the third and fourth generation" (Deut 5:9 NIV).

Carl Jung, a well-known psychoanalyst and probably the most theologically friendly among them, postulated that both the good and evil of previous generations is inherited from many generations. He called his theory "collective unconscious" and stated,

> This collective unconscious does not develop individually but is inherited. It consists of pre-existent forms, the archetypes, which can only become conscious secondarily and which give definite form to certain psychic contents.[2]

Although Jung did not discuss his theory in theological terms, he spoke of his view of the basic nature of the human. His basic assumption didn't significantly differ from that of Moses.

The concept of both individual and familial sin is critical to understanding the nature of brain work. The brain must grapple with what is conscious and what is unconscious. The "mind" as we understand it does not know the origins or even the presence of what is unconscious—but the brain does. Therefore, while a person is listening to a sermon, the brain brings up books from the dusty shelves of the library past, documentation long forgotten and some totally unknown to the conscious mind, and presents them in contrast, in agreement and in contradiction to what the brain is struggling with.

Is the worship service a time when preaching could redirect bodily and neurological energies toward seeking tranquility while being challenged with the seriousness of living by such words as the Sermon on the Mount? This rhetorical question can be answered, and the answer is yes. However, we must understand the nature of healing. It's necessary to keep the values of the word *healing* straight: wholeness, holiness, health, completeness (*holoklēria* in Greek). In the following chapters, brain work will become clearer and the specifics of utilizing brain energy will be elucidated.

6

Preaching Provides Brain Energy

The kingdom of God depends not on talk, but on power.

PAUL (1 COR 4:20)

Brain energy does not come from food and drink only, but also from what we think, what we read, the TV we watch, conversations we have, the environment, the symbols that surround us and the company we keep. Preaching in a sanctuary surrounded by symbols that unconsciously tie us to values and beliefs, words that enforce the environment and a congregation of people who reinforce the entire context are powerful sources of brain energy. Recent neurological findings support these statements.

In many instances, preaching has lost its energy-producing power. It has become a series of life illustrations pinpointed by loosely attached Scripture verses, relegating the sermon to a description of daily life. Positive, purposeful preaching is a pronouncement of biblical passages that aims their full impact on our daily lives. The Bible is described in this way: "The word of God is living and active, sharper than any two-edged sword, piercing until it divides soul from spirit, joints from marrow; it is able to judge the thoughts and intentions of the heart" (Heb 4:12). And "all scripture is inspired by God and is useful for teaching, for reproof, for correction, and for training in righteousness, so that everyone who belongs to God may be proficient, equipped for every good work" (2 Tim 3:16-17). Powerful preaching may start where we are but proceeds to where we need to be. Sermons are not attempts to make the Scriptures congruent with our lives but to make our lives congruent with the Scriptures.

Although all the sciences help us to understand and to preach more powerfully, there is no room to doubt where the real power comes from—God alone. Knowledge is only a tool to demonstrate that power. It is clear from the study of patriarchs of the church like John Calvin that knowledge of the sciences, although important, is of little value without the power of the Holy Spirit. He said, "Knowledge from the sciences is so much smoke without the heavenly science of Christ." In addition, he said, "Is it faith to understand nothing, and merely submit your convictions implicitly to the Church?" Like Calvin, we agree that we struggle for the balance of faith and science. Science is an *extension* not an *exchange* when preaching the Word of God.

Preaching is the power base of all that's done within and by the church. Preaching needs to be perceived, understood, practiced and appreciated for being *holy energy*, meaning that the power of preaching comes from an energy not defined by the words, the volume or range of voice, or the environment in which it is proclaimed. The universal energy directed by the Holy Spirit is hardly debatable. Scientists representing many different disciplines recognize universal energy and, whether properly credited or not, all energy is from God.

The scope of this book is much too narrow to entertain a discussion of energy medicine except to clarify that we do not need to understand energy based on modern conception of physics for it to be real. Furthermore, understanding other parts of God's creation does not reduce the power of the Christian message. Energy comes in many different forms, one of which is *spiritual* energy.

The Scriptures relate an incident that, if it occurred today, might well be classified as energy medicine. When the woman with the issue of blood (menometrorrhagia) for twelve years came to see Jesus, she was doubtless anemic, and an examination of her conjuctiva and fingernail beds would have revealed a pale, hemoglobin-deficient blood supply. Jesus did not touch her, nor did he know her presence in the very large crowd until he felt power going out from him and asked who had touched his clothes. (See Mk 5:25-34.)

Energy has oscillating characteristics, polarity, amplitude, waveform, frequency and many other parameters far beyond our current scientific understanding. For centuries, many modalities of healing have utilized applications of energy, some of which are understood while others are not. The practitioners did not categorize their healing in theological terms, nor do they now.

When leaving his disciples for the last time on earth, Jesus encouraged them, saying, "Very truly, I tell you, the one who believes in me will also do the works that I do and, in fact, will do greater works than these, because I am going to the Father" (Jn 14:12). This is an awesome and challenging passage in that the energy Jesus demonstrated is clearly available to those who believe. So the modern-day preacher can justly be challenged to find and employ this heavenly energy through the power of the Holy Spirit. It isn't sacrilegious to realize that God's energy that flowed through Christ also flows through his followers.

Dr. Ursula Anderson, a noted scholar, pediatrician, psychiatrist and public health authority, has capably discussed the power base of energy in her works, pointing out its power in health and healing, and as a potent tool against violence.[1] The recognition of energy is now accepted to the point that we have an entire new field of medicine called energy medicine, which utilizes unseen and previously unrecognized energy forms in practice. Anderson shows conclusively how energy fields flow through society—through the mother, teachers and healers—for good or for ill.

The concept of energy may seem strange to the minister, but understanding it is essential, since preachers are conduits of spiritual energy, recognized or not. Preaching not only *carries* an energy, it *is* energy—and that energy is powerful and far reaching. The preached Word is even more powerful when current knowledge of the sciences is employed for directed, purposeful ends.

Preaching may best be viewed in the light of the Old Testament prophets, who were often castigated, discredited, ostracized and even suffered physical torture and death at the hands of those who rejected their messages from God. The fact that even their enemies heard them and acted (albeit negatively) proves the dynamism and the power of the preached word (see 1 Kings 22; Jer 38).

John the Baptist gives us a perfect illustration of the proclaimer literally crying in the wilderness, preaching the kingdom of God. He was seen as a wild man, with a deranged mind, proclaiming a message that was foreign and unacceptable to many of his listeners. As a result, he was beheaded by the royalty of the day. Similarly, Paul the apostle preached to masses of people who rejected his gospel message, and his miseries at the hands of his enemies are legendary (2 Cor 11:23-25). The major lesson from these proclaimers is that the power of preaching is dynamic and moves an audience—sometimes to positive action and other times to negative action. But it always evokes a decision.

If the brain is to change, it requires persuasion. Some energy for change is intrinsic, such as pain. Pain can and does consciously and unconsciously force brain adaptations. Other energy comes from extrinsic sources, including preaching. "Along with most every marketing firm and politician in the world, psychologists have long been interested in understanding the mechanisms behind a persuasive argument . . . the medial prefrontal cortex, directly behind the eyes, and the precuneus, which sits near the back of the head." Neuroimaging suggests that these areas underpin self-reflection and likely are involved in decision making as a result of persuasion.[2] We have always known that people *can* be persuaded; now we know more *why* this is so.

The phrase *word power* came from a long-standing knowledge that words change people's lives. For preachers, this phrase has two very powerful meanings: (1) human words have human power to change people's lives, and (2) God's words have God's power to change people's lives. When combined, we must conclude that two elements are in simultaneous operation.

First, the power of any spoken word, when falling on receptive ears, is translated into meaning; meaning is translated into decision; and decision *can be* translated into action. But all information that becomes a decision is not necessarily transformed into action. The difference most often is the believability of the source of the information that encourages the decision and the willingness to accept the consequences of positive or negative action as a result of that decision. In this case, the preacher is the source—the power.

Second, when God's words (the Scriptures) are the power beneath the spoken word, the preacher becomes the anthropomorphized oracle of God. God sent Moses to the Israelites to establish the eternal "I am" of his message, and Moses began preaching in his stead (Ex 3:13-15). The preacher stands as the bodily, visible and authoritative messenger of information. God's announcement, "I am that I am," becomes the embodiment of the preacher as agent for God, which by virtue of God's authority *already* has meaning. The preacher therefore is not simply someone *speaking,* but someone functioning as the direct mouthpiece for God.

The concept of "announcement" as "embodiment" is a complex but basic brain phenomenon. The brain cannot process that which is strictly "ethereal" or "thought-based." Thoughts must have representation of some sort, usually something physical or at least phenomenological. For instance, God "announced" himself to the children of Israel in various ways, such as the burning bush (Ex

3:1-22), "a pillar of cloud by day" (Ex 13:21) and "a pillar of fire by night" (Ex 13:21). Since God was not physically visible nor present for auditory recognition, the "announcements" were "embodied" in physical manifestations. So it is with the Word as we know it today. God cannot be seen with physical eyes nor heard with physical ears (as many writers and poets have said in varying ways, "He has no hands but our hands, nor ears but our ears" [etc.]). The "announcement" is the "embodiment"—in this case, the minister's. And the embodiment is the announcement. The two cannot be separated.

Moses showed us the way as he passed the mantle of authority bestowed on him by God on to Joshua, as "the Lord commissioned Joshua" (see Deut 31:1-29). Some religious groups adhere to what is called *apostolic succession*, but even more important is *theistic authority*. Is this not a staggering thought that merits deep consideration of all who preach?

Preaching is not simply speaking. It is not entertainment. It is different from storytelling, giving a talk, making a speech or any other kind of public presentation. The homily, or sermon, is different from any other kind of communication. It presumes the power and authority of God and demands a kind of spiritual attention not required and not present in other settings. Preaching, like no other method of communication, is ordained by God for a special purpose. We do not need to wonder if a PowerPoint presentation would have been as powerful as Paul's sermon on Mars Hill. We do not decry or diminish technology, but God does not rely on it. The power is not in the method, but in the message.

The preacher is set apart from the congregation, yet is very much a part of it. Through ordination, the minister is set apart for the preaching of the gospel and with that ordination comes the public recognition of a *divine call* to represent the kingdom of God in the here and now. As any representative of a higher authority (such as an ambassador or emissary) must carry the message faithfully, so must the clergy as the ordained representatives of God on earth.

The power of the position does not come from the person, but from the authority behind the person.

So with clergy, the authority is from God by the enabling power of the Holy Spirit. The preacher is God's agent. Although as believers we have individual responsibility and direct access to God through Christ, God has ordained those who serve as preachers with a *different* level of responsibility, accountability and agency. To be an *agent* is to be authoritative, responsible and accountable. It is not to be taken lightly.

Preaching is a necessary agency of the church, and preachers are its agents.

> [Preaching] is as old as the Bible itself (2 Peter 2:5). It is a necessary adjunct of a religion that is communicated to man by means of an objective and authoritative revelation, such as we have in the sacred Scriptures, . . . that faith is disseminated by means of teaching through argument, motive and exhortation. The agency for the spread of a religion of persuasion must be preaching.[3]

This awesome task is understood but often minimized by those wearing "the cloth." Among the members of the congregation, it is even less emphasized. The power of preaching must be considered within the *ethics* of ministry. What is the intended end of preaching? Is it primarily to increase church membership? Is it to gain attendees for greater financial coffers? Is it to attain grandiosity and fame for the preacher? Is it to produce other self-aggrandizing results?

Ethos, Ethic and Ethics

If preachers do not examine the very ethos, ethic and ethics of their profession, who should? "Walking the talk," "role modeling" and a plethora of other phrases could illustrate the role of clergy. The terms *ethos, ethic* and *ethics* will be discussed at length later in this book, but at this point it's imperative to understand that integrity and the ability to demonstrate that integrity is essential to preaching.

The clergy in every society throughout history has been entrusted with imparting wisdom. The philosophical and pragmatic basis of wisdom is found in the "soul" of the person and the organization that seeks to impart it. The core (*ethos*) of that person and organization demonstrates the ethos (essential nature), while the actions of that person or organization demonstrate the ethic (true intent), and the methods reveal the actual ethics. The preacher and the church exhibit (or fail to exhibit) the ethical ability to impart wisdom.

The words *wisdom* and *discernment* get tossed around easily, but their meanings are ambiguous to most people. The Bible's Wisdom books are full of admonitions regarding wisdom. Proverbs 9:10 reminds us that "the fear of the LORD is the *beginning* of wisdom" (emphasis added). Knowledge and proper respect for God are the foundation, and when it is properly laid, additional knowledge may be added to the wisdom base. In his writings to the church at Corinth, Paul reminded them of the theological foundation when he stated that Christ is "the wisdom of God" (1 Cor 1:24). Both of these Scriptures and many more underline the necessity of a solid theological base for any added knowledge.

Further, knowledge without that base is simply knowledge, not wisdom. The clergyperson, by designation of that office, is expected to be able to *discern*, meaning to judge clearly and to have an acute understanding of the most wise and prudent among a myriad of desirable options. It could rightly be said that wisdom is the ability to utilize knowledge in a timely, adroit and appropriate manner.

Both individual and public good are placed in the hands of the preacher because of an assumed divine ethos and the willingness of the church to participate in God's work with the ethic and ethics of higher spiritual authority. The supporting church system is given the authority to impact intellectual, moral and spiritual changes in its subjects. Ministers purport to be doing good and representing the kingdom. They *are* what they *do*, and they *do* as they *are*. When authenticity is defined in this way, that means many clergy (and laity) are inauthentic. Many structural elements within denominational systems promote inauthenticity, and unfortunately the public often buys an inauthentic product.

So, what does this have to do with theology or neurobiological aspects of the brain and of preaching? The brain is consistent in its acceptance and assimilation of its own definition of perceived truth. Long before financial and personal scandals are made public, the intuitive congregant recognizes that something is wrong. The lack of authenticity comes through in ways unrecognized by the preacher. The choice of words, the subliminal messages, the slight changes in affect, the minor shifts in focus and much more alerts the astute parishioner to an underlying discrepancy.

Also needed is *fiduciary responsibility*. The church and its clergy are public fiduciaries, meaning that they are entrusted with both spoken and unspoken responsibility for truth, the sacred good of a community, financial integrity and personal morality.

To have integrity, the message and the messenger of the church must be authentic, frugal, effective, sustainable and reproducible. Does contemporary, organized Christianity fulfill these requirements? Let's look at each of these attributes. Is the church authentic or simply giving the appearance of such? Is the current representation of Christendom frugal rather than wasteful? There can be little doubt about the inconsistency of the church's effectiveness. Among all the attributes, its sustainability is the least doubted. The church has lasted through thick and thin. It is also clearly reproducible. And although it may have difficulty from age to age in a given geographic locale, it seems that the church prospers. Today it is in trouble in the Western Hemisphere but rebounding with vigor in Asia.

Preaching that is powerful rests on a carefully designed epistemology (a theory of knowledge) and consistent hermeneutic
(method of interpretation). To develop an epistemology and hermeneutic for an ethical parish ministry, we must start with a view
of the human in need of much more than humanness. We must
build on what we know by gleaning from science and Scripture
regarding humans. Approaching preaching armed with what we
already know only limits us; if we believe that our knowledge is
accurate and complete, new discoveries can't be activated, due to
the closed systems we have established. Faith is what allows the
wedding of the scientifically known and the scripturally known.
What is scientifically known changes in every generation; the
Christian message does not. An expanding knowledge of the
human and a biblically based theology is the basis of power in
preaching. Preaching includes the evolving application of a constant truth, not an evolving truth with a consistent application.
The method does and should change; the message does not.

Understanding what we know and what we do not know is
crucial. Accepting by faith a reality that we verbally affirm in creeds
is critical. Further, utilizing what we do know in an intelligent
manner combined with believing and proclaiming what God tells
us is true in the Scriptures are the basis of rational sermonizing.
The power is found in the ability to arrest a hearer's attention on
both the seen and the unseen, on both experiential knowledge and
faith. Although faith is based on the "evidence of things not seen"
(Heb 11:1 KJV), it does not preclude increasing our faith by adding
evidence from what is seen. Faith is not diminished by knowledge,
since our knowledge is always incomplete; it is magnified by what
the soul knows to be true, with or without scientific knowledge.

Preaching is indeed powerful; it constantly and incessantly
changes minds and lives, more than most of us comprehend.

7

Brain Stimuli Produce Behavioral Responses

The test of the worth of a preacher is when his congregation (goes) away saying, not "what a beautiful sermon." But "I will do something."

ST. FRANCIS DE SALES (1567–1622)

It is impossible for the brain to receive external stimuli without producing a behavioral response. The response may be to accept, to reject, to file away for future reference or to make an immediate decision. How we behave is based on what we believe, and what we believe is based on what we already believe plus new stimuli. John Buchanan, former pastor of the Fourth Presbyterian Church in Chicago, speaks pointedly about preaching for decision: "If we wrap up the Sunday morning service without posing a question to be answered, a challenge or an invitation, we have left critical work undone."[1]

Intentional preaching demands a response. In fact, preaching always results in a response, demanded or not. We have learned how the brain processes information and determines what to do with it. We now know from neurobiology that not to make a decision is an impossibility. The brain can't refuse information. It can, however, refuse to assimilate and/or accommodate it, which results not in refusal of the hearing or the listening but in assignment to a pathway that will end either in stagnant storage or in an en-grammed pathway for selective use in decision making. In lay terms, we call this process a decision to deny or reject what has been preached or a decision to think about it. However, there is always a decision. Purposeful preaching moves listeners toward an *intentional* decision.

Therefore, preaching is not an argument; it is not a discussion; it is not an interlude between other parts of the service. It is the introduction of information into an already prepared brain for acceptance or for discarding into the mental trash can. We now know that the brain is incapable of shutting out stimuli arriving through the auditory route. It is embedded deeply within the brain and is processed within the context of all that is already there. This is why preaching should occur regularly and should build on what hearers have stored in their *physical* brains, which will produce *emotional* results.

There are many differing conceptions of the decision made as a result of preaching. Some limit the decision to whether the hearer is converted. No one doubts the value of this; however, it ignores the many other decisions Christians must make to continue to grow in wisdom and grace. And all these decisions need scriptural support. Knowing the needs of the congregation allows for person-alizing sermons. The competent minister is aware of individual and corporate needs and *intentionally* focuses on them. Gener-alized sermons can reap generalized results, which brings us to the question of demonstrable outcome. In most professional fields, practitioners must be able to demonstrate measurable outcomes. Are there, should there be, and indeed can there be measurements for the ministry? If not, why not?

Even the mind at rest, or for that matter asleep, is making deci-sions. Listening may stop, but the brain keeps working. It is like a giant warehouse with a line of eighteen-wheeler tractor-trailers filled with merchandise constantly unloading. The brain must decide how to catalog the inventory, where to store it and what retrieval system to put into place for immediate recall when needed.

If the preacher keeps this in mind, it will be helpful. The parishioner is sitting in the pew with both old and new information being poured into her or his brain. Even inventory that was not ordered but arrives must be unloaded, cataloged, stored and made ready for recall. Recall does not necessarily mean *positive* recall. The listener may recall the information as superfluous, boring or even incorrect. Upon immediate appraisal, memory comes into play and helps with the process. If the parishioner has had negative experiences with sermons previously, the clerk unloading the inventory may place it in the damaged goods room. If the parishioner has had positive experiences, the information is likely to be put in the "ready for use" room.

Here, *religare* is once again pertinent. Whether it is good or bad things we are reminded of, we tie back to them. When bad things happen, often the mind regresses to a previous experience and tells itself, consciously or unconsciously, "yes, I deserve that," and prepares for the expected punishment. Or, when the mind ties back to a pleasant experience, it prepares itself for reward. We can substitute knowledge for feeling, but in the long run, feelings always win—even when they are wrong—because they allow the mind to regress to reward or punishment.

In preaching, we must remind the listener that feelings are just that, and although the feelings are real, the truth may well be elsewhere. Even when feelings represent truthful happenings, they are always diminished or exaggerated over time; they are never perfect, even in the moment of the event. They are always contaminated by the past and rearranged to fit the expectations of the future. So we can't trust feelings totally; we must balance feelings with truth, thus making decisions based on reasonable and real knowledge and present circumstances.

When under attack, the adult mind regresses to the security of infantile memories. This is an interesting thought when we consider a "hellfire and brimstone" sermon and try to reconcile it with our infantile memory of "Jesus Loves Me."

Preachers preach to all sorts of minds, frequently without knowing much, if anything, of the listeners' backgrounds. The vocabulary, analogies, metaphors, illustrations and interpretations of the Scripture meet a wide spectrum of memories and experiences. Preachers who use only the newer translations of the Scriptures, for instance, may miss the opportunity to connect with older worshipers who resonate with the King James Version. That's the version they learned in Sunday school and the one from which they memorized Bible verses. The preacher who uses only the King James Version may entirely miss the target of the younger set, who doesn't relate to the archaic King James language. Yet who can deny that when the Twenty-Third Psalm is to be read, the King James Version is often requested.

Determining how and why individuals choose as they do is not merely a mind game, but is a solid basis for theologically educating parishioners. Although the precise neurological process by which decisions are made is still unknown, this much we know:

- We decide by associating new choices with previous ones—ones that brought pleasure are grounds to accept new choices that are consonant with previous ones (apt to bring pleasure).

- We decide by conditioning—repetitive information that is compatible with our intellectual skills. We can delay gratification if conditioned to do so.

- We decide by looking for peer acceptance or rejection. Even nongratifying decisions are made when accompanied by peer approval.

- We decide based on our most primitive instincts related to reward and punishment. The concepts of heaven and hell are theological illustrations of this point.

Being adept, thoughtful and a careful planner, the preacher can choose tools much as any other skilled artisan would. Those who know how to preach only one way are like the carpenter who has only a hammer and therefore all problems must be nails. The preacher may be pounding on what appears to be a nail but is a glass window. The sermon will evoke a decision, but it may be to discard the broken glass.

But rest assured that decisions will be made. Some would look forward to the next sermon, and some would decide never to listen to that preacher again. Paul's words to the Corinthians seem to apply to this issue: "In the church I would rather speak five intelligible words to instruct others than ten thousand words in a tongue" (1 Cor 14:19 NIV).

PURPOSEFUL PREACHING PREPARES THE WAY FOR THE NEXT SERMON
Preaching sets the stage for the next sermon, but most parishioners won't remember the connection. The mind looks for connections, but not usually from one sermon to the next unless the sequence is carefully laid out and explained, with prompts along the way. The brain is capable of thinking in outline form, but does not usually do so unless specifically directed. Sermons may be seen as individual lectures, so the hearer's brain puts a period at the end of each one; or they may be considered as partial information, with a semicolon to anticipate the completion of the idea.

Careful planning leads to sequential proclamations. Such planning is not simply to make sermons logistically, contextually or literarily attractive. Carefully planned and executed sermons allow the brain to move from concept to concept, adding new information to what has already been accepted. Sermons given as isolated, individual messages force the brain to work much harder in relocating and reattaching information, thus requiring much greater memory—and motivation. When the brain can attain more with less effort, it will. As a congregant hears, his or her mind is building a storehouse of information. This information is combined in a series of exclamation points, question marks and ruminations. The brain continues to sort out thinking and give meaning to what was preached, and it is orderly in the final analysis, according to the orientation of that individual brain.

Schoolteachers and college professors understand the need for lesson plans and course outlines. These keep both the teacher and the student on track and allow for teaching precept upon precept and the student learning incremental knowledge based on already assimilated information. Should preaching require any less?

There are many very practical reasons for planning a sermon series. Some of these may be scoffed at by the unknowing, but not by honest preachers. They include avoiding the necessity for Saturday-night sermon cramming, developing a series of sermons that build on each other, creating a worship year that provides an emphasis for the congregation, coordinating hymns and music with the sermon theme and allowing for suspense and "to be continued" interest.

Some argue that such planning thwarts spontaneity and the work of the Spirit. How omnipotent of us to assume that any of our planning is so powerful. As essential as humility is to the success of any preaching, an argument may be made to do things in the church "decently and in order" (1 Cor 14:40). Orderliness helps the brain sort information, as it is constantly searching for consistency, continuity and closure. A purposefully planned program of preaching leads to sequential information that helps the brain to follow and to find the closure it seeks.

Vocabulary, syntax, grammar and delivery style are important. Great words are easily lost because of the words chosen, a regional or ethnic incongruity or a poor preaching voice or style. Again, this is not a book on *how* to preach, but a discussion of what the brain does with preaching, whether we want it to or not.

When Paul wrote of speaking words from his rational mind

rather than in an unknown tongue, he may have been referring to glossolalia or to any kind of preaching that hearers are not able to understand (1 Cor 14:2). Vocabulary that forces the mind away from the message dilutes the power. Themes and vocabulary that encourage a structured process of thinking promote the power behind the message rather than promoting the power of the speaker.

Preachers find that a continuity of themes encourages attendance. When a theme is presented in mind-engaging ways, interest grows and attendees become curious about what comes next. The end of a sermon becomes the beginning of the next, and the next sermon lightly reviews the last, since the brain responds to re-engagement of terms and thought patterns and then moves on to receive new material.

There are many methods of ensuring a purposeful sequence in leading a congregation. Experienced clergy have far more methods than can be mentioned here. The following are given only as ideas for those who might need them: preaching through a book of the Bible, following a lectionary, using a themed or goal-driven sequence, educating for stewardship, instructing for discipleship, addressing the mission of the church or preparing for missional endeavors. There are doubtless many more methods that permit the brain to integrate new information based on what it has already learned.

Further, attention must be paid to the stewardship of time—the time of the preacher and the time of the listeners. For example, if a minister preaches for twenty minutes to one hundred listeners, the time stewardship is two thousand minutes, or slightly over thirty-three hours. Rarely is the stewardship of time conceptualized in this fashion. Thinking of it as such reveals the large amount of time permitted by congregants for either edification or questionable use.

Not knowing how the learning process of humans operates is no longer excusable. We would not tolerate a medical professional who does not stay abreast of how the body works and how medicine interacts with it. Why should the religious world not expect the same level of dedicated knowledge from the clergy? The neuroscience of human learning, patterns of memory, methods of information retention, attention spans and other factors relating to how parishioners listen, hear, think and remember are available in lay language to clergy and laypeople alike. Ministers who do not consider this knowledge may be less informed of their primary task than their parishioners are.

The preacher assumes and hopes that her or his sermon will be remembered over the long term, which requires short-term memory too. According to neuroscientist E. Kandel,

> In understanding long-term memory [the next step] was to understand how it becomes firmly established, a process called consolidation. For a memory to persist, the incoming information must be thoroughly and deeply processed. This is accomplished by attending to the information and associating it meaningfully and systematically with knowledge already well established in memory.[2]

This admonition is helpful in understanding the necessity of repetition, or *religare,* and the use of every brain gate possible for preaching.

As with many topics mentioned in this book, sufficient space can't be given even for a modest discussion of what we know about learning, motivation and brain function. We do know that purposeful preaching must be intentional, directional, well conceived and competently delivered. The motivated clergyperson will study to build these preaching competencies. Peter reminded church leaders, "Feed the flock of God which is among you, taking the oversight thereof, not by constraint, but willingly; not for filthy lucre, but of a ready mind" (1 Pet 5:2 KJV).

Preaching and Pastoring Are Different

Being a good preacher and being an effective pastor are very different, require different skills and support each other. Effective preaching is the foundation for successful pastoring, and being an effective pastor encourages listeners to "hear" the preaching.

Preaching and pastoring are distinctly different; in fact, they are two different, though closely related, functions. The word *pastoring* does not appear in the dictionary, but has a clearer meaning than the designation "being a pastor"; the latter being a noun, which is important, but does not convey the gerund form—the constant, continuous, active work of being a pastor. Performing the tasks of being a pastor requires a different mindset and commitment than simply holding the designated position. The tasks of being a pastor go with the position, but the position does not guarantee the accomplishment of the tasks.

For example, without purposeful preaching, pastoring becomes religiously oriented social work. It has only the energy and power of the social and psychological dimension and requires no biblical or theological knowledge. Such activity is also devoid of the demonstrations of grace (Communion, baptism and so on) proclaimed by Christian theology. Since pastoring is the *care of souls*, it demands a power and an energy commensurate with the needs of the soul. The pastor who only preaches may not be giving sufficient attention to the care of souls. However, the pastor who neglects the power of preaching limits his or her ability to properly pastor—that is, to shepherd the flock.

Confidence, trust and relationship come from both preaching and pastoring. Neither can be neglected, since they are both essential bases for healing, not only within the context of pain and suffering but also within the context of healing the human relationship within the divine purpose. The pastor who preaches powerfully cares for souls against the backdrop of Spirit-driven energy that provides the structural dynamic that can reconcile sin and grace. *Preaching is the proclamation of the Word. Pastoring is delivering that proclamation to the soul.*

Many parishioners say their minister is a good preacher; others say their minister is a good pastor. Far fewer say their minister is both. The skills for preaching and the skills for pastoring are very different. They are frequently seen as two different vocations rather than as extensions of each other. Good pastoring makes for good sermons, and good sermons make for good pastoring. Pastoring is the application of the preaching, and preaching is the basis for the pastoring.

Preaching for healing is carrying the word in the pulpit to the hospital bedside or counseling room, with the underlying knowledge of how God uses the mind to heal the body. The sermon energy from the pulpit is taken to the conference room with the underlying knowledge of how God uses the Word to bring meaning to words (even conflict) to encourage mind-changing decisions. The minister also takes the preached word to communities in conflict, to organizations that deny justice, to businesses that cheat their employees and to governments that are at war. Preaching for healing is comprehensive. The preacher who has a solid grasp on preaching as healing anticipates the opportunities to apply the preached word as pastoring in the marketplace.

Likewise, the minister who has pastored faithfully has a quiver full of real-life illustrations that take the Word from the page to the heart. These stories are not parables or fairytales; they come from the congregation, from the community and from the everyday experiences of real people living real lives. The struggles amplify the meaning of the Word, and the Word amplifies the meaning of being a pastor as well as a preacher.

The pastoring task is huge. It entails hospital visitation, prison ministry and counseling the married, the soon-to-be married and the soon-to-be divorced. It includes listening to the heartbreaking stories of parents who have lost a child to cancer, to the elderly who have lived a fruitful life and are ready to pass on into eternity, and to those who have not lived a fruitful life but are dying anyway. The list goes on and on.

The question is, From where does the clergyperson derive the strength to share with others? From the preached Word. What has been proclaimed is now embodied in the *preaching pastor*, and the minister is then seen as the *pastoring preacher*—both consistent with a positive, purposeful ministry.

To some, preaching comes easier than pastoring; to others, pastoring is easier than preaching. Both demand an acknowledgement of fundamental beliefs. The minister moving among the flock knows what has been preached and what the flock has confessed to believe, thus establishing a framework for immediate pastoral work. A counselor or pastor who meets someone in need for the first time must establish rapport and a basis of trust. The preacher who has done the job well from the pulpit is many steps ahead, having already established a belief base and a rapport base from which to further the demonstration of God's grace.

Preaching and pastoring demonstrate different things. Preaching invites attendees to hear and listen to the encouragement, admonitions, blessings and benedictions of the clergy. However, in pastoring the attendees see these messages in full operation. The preacher who has put the two together allows for true religion to take place. Again, we learn the new by tying it back to the old. Now we can see the importance of this neurobiological fact. The preacher who has faithfully preached has the opportunity to bring the truth of God's peace, forgiveness, love and other aspects of the gospel to the one being pastored, because there is something to tie it back to. This brings joy and reward to the pastor, who now sees the fruit of having established a cognitive faith basis on which to build hope and grace in the time of need. As Jesus proclaimed, "The Spirit of the Lord is upon me, because he hath anointed me to preach the gospel to the poor; he hath sent me to heal the brokenhearted, to preach deliverance to the captives, and recovering of sight to the blind, to set at liberty them that are bruised" (Lk 4:18 KJV).

CHARACTERISTICS OF PREACHERS WHO ATTRACT "CUSTOMERS"

Although there are doubtless many reasons why some churches thrive and others don't, a study of church history shows that the powerful preacher always creates a significant place in the community. In this day of dwindling church attendance, clergy are largely still respected. Even after all the scandals and improprieties well reported and embellished by the media, this is still true.

The total power of preaching may not be seen simply in the number of attendees at services; however, like any other invention, a better mousetrap still captures more mice. When preaching no longer meets the needs of those who hear it, they will cease to attend to it; they may still respect the minister but reject the church. As a matter of fact, they will treat it as they would a mousetrap—buying it when needed. They figure the church has always been there and will be there when needed for a wedding, a funeral or a place to go on Easter or Christmas.

In today's world, there is widespread discouragement about the church, even among the faithful. Many feel that it no longer meets the needs of our fast-paced, technologically driven society. Those who are unchurched see little reason for belonging to one. Our age is one of amplified hedonism and immediate self-gratification. It may well be that our age is advanced in focusing on self-centered needs, but every age has had its own challenges. The church faces those challenges, and the church is still in existence. There were great preachers in all ages who helped to change people's lives and the face of communities. We also have no scriptural indication that the Word would become less powerful as the ages roll on. We have the same scriptural assurance that our predecessors had, and the challenges are only different verses of the same song.

The attempt to reduce the preached word and expand the entertainment aspects of the church service may not be the answer, but instead part of the problem. Catering to what others want may only prove to them and to us that we are hypocrites, since we know the difference between want and need. Children know their parents are fools when they give them candy right before supper. Do parishioners know that they have duped the preacher?

Charles Haddon Spurgeon, John Wesley, Dwight L. Moody, Pope John Paul II, Bishop Fulton Sheen, Billy Graham, Martin Luther King Jr., George Buttrick, Henry Sloane Coffin, Harold J. Ockenga and many other great preachers share a number of admirable similarities. Though they were from different theological positions, used different preaching methods, had different denominational ties and were from different ethnic roots, we can learn much from these giants:

- They preached strong, uncompromising sermons.
- They included traditional music that all could relate to.
- They were powerful orators.
- They attracted huge crowds.

- They appealed to both interdenominational and nondenominational audiences.

- They did not become known as "in it for the money."

- They consistently brought audiences to a decision.

- They encouraged whole communities toward salvation and right living.

- They hold a place in history as powerful leaders.

- They are still studied today by aspiring clergy.

Professor Thomas Long at Emory's Candler School of Theology wrote cogently, "Like other teachers of preaching, I listen to a lot of sermons, sometimes a dozen in a single day. I have noticed that this fact rarely evokes covetous sighs from my faculty colleagues, many of whom imagine a daily regimen of multiple homilies akin to endless trips to the periodontist."[1] Granted, they are listening to students who are preparing to become preachers, but we all know that many professional preachers do little if any better.

After listening to preachers of many different denominations and having been a preacher for over sixty years, I find the following observations by Keith Drury to be particularly cogent. According to him, these are the twenty-one skills of great preachers:

The one thing most of us would rather do than preach is hear another great preacher. I mean a "Great" preacher. I've learned plenty from hearing the best preachers, especially in a live setting. For most of my life, when sitting under a great preacher, I've taken dual sets of notes, including content on one list, and a separate set of notes on their communication skills. What have I discovered in these 40 years worth of notes? Here's my summary:

- Content: All of my "Great Preachers" had something to say. Even as "great communicators," they didn't substitute style for substance.

- Passion: The best Preachers I've heard had a passion for what they said which seemed to spring from a general spiritual burden for people, which is different from just loving to preach. Messages are easier to love than people.

- Credibility: Great Preachers practice what they preach—"they live it." "Great Communicators" might get away with all kinds of private sin, but not truly "Great Preachers." I've had to downgrade some of my "Great Preachers" to "Great Communicators" over the last few decades.

- Prepared: Great Preachers don't "wing it"—even if the people couldn't tell. (They can.)

- Notes: Most Great Preachers limited their use of notes. Thanks to TV, preachers can no longer read to a crowd with their nose buried in their notes.

- Simple: Great Preachers have a way of bringing high truths down to the bottom shelf, yet without compromising the greatness of truth. In this they are like Jesus. People don't leave a truly great preacher saying, "Boy, he's smart." They say, "Now I understand."

- Short: While Great Preachers are able to hold your attention in a preaching marathon, most were able to also preach a great sermon in 30 minutes or less. (I don't know about you, but I've discovered that 30 minutes is plenty of time for a preacher to give a sermon, except in the few instances when I myself am the preacher.)

- Convicting: People hear God prick their conscience when Great Preachers preach. They give more than a "sermon" or "talk"—they deliver a "message" from God.

- Self-revealing: Great Preachers know how to tell personal stories on themselves. They become real to their listeners. Yet they do this while avoiding the egocentric

self-absorption of many pop preachers who make themselves the subject of the sermon instead of God.

- Confidence: Great Preachers don't seem scared. Maybe
  they are, but they never seem to show it.

- Tone: While the great preachers of the past often thun-
  dered out salvos like giant cannons, the Great Preachers
  of today almost all use a conversational tone of voice.
  They know that people today don't listen to speakers
  who shout.

- Story-telling: All Great Preachers through history have
  this trait in common: they are good storytellers. That goes
  for both telling story illustrations and direct Bible stories.

- Prop: I've noticed that some Great Preachers use an object
  or prop to get their truth across—usually an ordinary thing
  like a salt shaker, a packet of yeast, or a glass of water.

- Humor: Many Great Preachers are funny, though not all of
  them. The humorous preachers are able to "get them back"
  after they've been on a roll, so that the message can stay
  central, not the humor. Those who can't keep the message
  central are merely "Great Communicators" or "Christian
  Humorists," not "Great Preachers."

- Pace: Even fast-paced Great Preachers use pauses where
  you can catch your breath. The listener then can digest
  their last few bites of truth without bolting the whole meal
  down undigested. Many Great Preachers follow the traditional [African-American] pace in the poem: "Begin low;
  Continue slow; Rise up higher; Catch on fire; Sit down in
  the storm."

- Eyes: Great Preachers keep their eyes glued to their audience. Each person in the congregation feels the preacher
  is "looking right at me."

- Fast on feet: Most Great Preachers are able to work in the surprises in a service like thunder, scratching on the roof, sirens, etc.

- Intensity: The Great Preachers I've heard varied their intensity—sometimes they were louder, then they'd get as soft as a whisper, sometimes they'd be so intense that my own stomach would ache, then they'd drop back and adopt a tender or even chuckling style.

- Movement: Most Great Preachers I've heard used their bodies to preach along with their words. They seemed to intuitively know that a congregation is getting a full 55 percent of the communication from their facial gestures and body movement.

- Decision: My Great Preachers never gave a message and walked away. They called for my specific and personal decision in response to God's truth. They preached for decision, not for entertainment or education. Perhaps I call them "Great" partially because God changed me under their influence.

- Landing: All the really Great Preachers I've heard were able to land their message on the first pass. Most lesser preachers circle the airport several times before bringing it in, or (worse still) do several "touch-and-go's" before landing. You know, it's a funny thing—I can always see when the other guy should land his sermon, better than knowing when to bring my own message down on the runway.[2]

It has yet to be proven that great preaching will not attract audiences. It's being regularly proven that mediocre preaching coupled with unfamiliar music and poor pastoring fails. Of course, we can point to megachurches that seem to have succeeded in spite of paying attention to little if any of this discourse. Grace and peace to those who have done well. However, for every one of the successful ones, there are thousands of struggling, dying congregations. There is no doubt a place for both in our needy world.

Megachurches demonstrate the point well that the world will beat a path to better mousetraps. But the megachurch in its current form may not be all that it seems. Remember, the first mouse gets caught; the second mouse gets the cheese. In its first iteration, the megachurch may not be providing the cheese. But megachurches have clearly demonstrated many things, including that many worshipers want something different than they are getting in traditional churches. If the megachurch philosophy and traditional church philosophy could get together, they might indeed invent a better mousetrap.

In his book *Have a Little Faith*, Mitch Albom tells of a rabbi whose sermons were so arresting that "you could glance around the room and see that no one looked away; even when he was scolding them, they were riveted. Honestly, you exhaled when he finished; that's how good he was."[3] From experience, theology and neurobiology, we know that the mind attends to what is compelling and has relevancy for peace, preservation and hope.

Great orators and preachers have always drawn huge crowds to hear them. In *Giants*, John Stauffer recounted how Frederick Douglass went into a "ramshackle old post office, orating for abolition. . . . Within two weeks his listeners had grown from five to five thousand."[4] Granted, he was preaching against slavery, a political issue, but wasn't it very theological as well? Nonetheless, doesn't the modern-day preacher have topics as vibrant, controversial and theologically demanding? Maybe the better question is, Does the church have nothing to be passionate about?

The argument could be made that preachers who do not soothe or "psychologize" their audience do not attract customers. But history doesn't bear this out to be true. Many of the nation's largest congregations have been built on "hellfire and brimstone" preaching. Many of the great revivals of the world were instigated by fiery preaching. One of the most memorable sermons of all time is "Sinners in the Hands of an Angry God," belted out by Jonathan Edwards, a passionate preacher and intellectual who later became president of what is now Princeton University. Although this book is not promoting a specific kind of preaching, it's certain that the preacher needs to determine early on whether the sermon is directed only at the intellectual individual or only at the emotional person, or at both. Great preachers seem to be able to address both in the same sermon.

Whether we choose to follow one theological path or another, the truth remains that people want to "hear it like it is" and are quick to know if they are being coddled and mollified instead of confronted. The subconscious mind knows the difference, and it is much more powerful than the conscious mind. Eventually the mind gets bored when it's being caressed rather than cared for. Thomas Long says, "One thing we are waiting for is for preachers who feel the strong wind, who sense the heights above them and the abyss below and take a deep breath and preach a life-changing gospel."[5]

Getting to the Brain with Theology

*All that the L*ORD *speaketh, that I must do.*

BALAAM (NUM 23:26 KJV)

Theology is unique in that everyone either believes or believes not to believe. The brain is energized by theology—whether believed or not—and with effective preaching, it is thrown into debate with itself. The neural pathways of memory are activated, while the cortex and social-behavioral parts of the brain are stimulated and forced to deal with new and old information. There are few other forms of communication that excite, stimulate, anger and appease the brain all at the same time.

THE CHURCH HAS MANY POWERFUL INSTRUMENTS FOR HEALING
Since the first Christian assembly, many techniques (sacraments) have been established for the institution, enrichment and empowerment of the faith. Some have survived argumentative dissensions, although many have fallen by the wayside. For purposes of this discussion, a very broad definition of *sacrament* will be used. Some contemporary assemblies barely recognize these deeply rooted traditions, thus robbing themselves of their benefits. These sacraments may well be considered "demonstrations of grace."

The powerful, purposeful practitioner of preaching harnesses all of the tools available. Throughout the centuries, many of these tools have been discouraged, and many have been abandoned. Again, an essential and powerful tool is preaching directly from the Scriptures, punctuated by applications from real life. There are many other practices within the church that provide emphasis and support to the message.

The more common demonstrations of grace are considered here, but many more could be included. Some, although powerful, are barely more than idiosyncrasies of Christian assemblies, but are of great value nonetheless. Further, it behooves creative preachers to find methods to support their ministry of preaching.

Whether these are called methods of grace, sacraments, memorials or simply practices makes little difference to the average layperson. Only the ecclesiastically trained mind argues the definition. For the purposes of this book, they are considered important gates to the brain. To the average churchgoer, these words are palindromes—whatever you call them, they are the same backward or forward. For example, from the theological point of view, we can argue about the method of baptism, but for this writing, the *purpose* of baptism is the same.

Dealing with theological differences regarding these practices can be like talking in a foreign language. Whether we call it a *chien* or a *perro*, it is still a dog. To most people, these are demonstrations of God's forgiveness and love, whatever they are called. All that's done in God's name is sacramental. Preaching and its ministrations are best received by the average mind when devoid of excessive "ivory tower" argumentation and loaded with everyday meaning. In the final analysis, the mind operates on pragmatism; therefore, it's best to leave definitions to those who need them for theological, ecclesiological or political purposes.

CONFESSION

Although some religious bodies—primarily Roman Catholic, historical Anglican and Eastern Orthodox—have maintained confession as a tool for healing, Protestant groups have largely abandoned the practice. Technically speaking, the Anglican Church differs in that "auricular confession" is the Rite of Reconciliation, and by edict of Elizabeth I, "All may, none must, and some ought" to attend to that sacrament.[1] The Roman Catholic Church has continuously and faithfully employed this sacrament, and there is no doubt that many have found healing, reconciliation and hope in it.

The theological reasons for retaining or abandoning confession are not the point of this discussion. No one with Christian theology denies the *value* of confession; the disagreement is over *to whom* the confession should be made. We all agree that "if we confess our sins, he who is faithful and just will forgive us our sins and cleanse us from all unrighteousness" (1 Jn 1:9). Further, there are many forms and venues for confession—some in private, some in counseling, some to a pastor or priest, some public—but in the final analysis, all are made to God.

Solid scientific psychology has verified the power of confession and has developed many systems of counseling and psychotherapy predicated on the concept of confession and forgiveness. Beginning with Freud's "father confessor" and continuing through psychologists and psychiatrists today, patients (penitents) unburden themselves to their doctors (priests). Although many of the basic premises of Freudian psychoanalysis are theologically questionable (and in some cases diametrically opposed to Christian theology), the practice of confessional psychotherapy has proven effective. Freud called this "the *method of catharsis* (purification)."[2]

Many recent publications in the field of "spiritual psychology" have given voice to the value of confession under the label of "spiritually oriented psychotherapy." As valuable as such is, its fatal flaw is the assumption that simply verbalizing erroneous commissions or omissions eradicates them. To some extent, that has proven valuable from the purely psychological point of view. However, few people believe that a psychologist or psychiatrist is capable of forgiving sin. This is where the minister, who stands in representation for God, is uniquely equipped to lead the penitent into God's forgiveness. Not a small difference.

Although many arguments may be made as to the scriptural basis, or lack thereof, for confessing sins in any place other than privacy, the power of relational declaration of wrongdoing and recognition of its consequences is indeed meaningful when confessed openly. If for no other reason (and there are many credible reasons), confession may be seen legitimately as a strong tool for the church in healing. Underlying the very basics of psychoanalysis is the necessity of eradicating one's secret or hidden feelings via abreaction—"bringing into conscious recollection previously repressed or unpleasant experiences that have been buried in the unconscious"[3] and verbally *confessing* inner conflicts.

There is not sufficient reason to doubt the value of confession. Unfortunately, confession to non-clergy professionals is bereft of the power of the gospel. There is a major difference in the authority basis between a non-clergy professional who accepts transgressions with neutrality and clergy who are able to pronounce, "If we confess our sins, he who is faithful and just will forgive us our sins and cleanse us from all unrighteousness" (1 Jn 1:9), and "Through Jesus Christ, your sins are forgiven" (compare Luke 5:20). There is no contest; sacred authority has no equal.

FORGIVENESS

Nowhere in the world is there a more profound demonstration of "being forgiven" than in the church. Forgiveness uniquely belongs to the practice of faith. And although some psychological practices speak of forgiveness, apart from understanding the divine, such practices are empty and their shallowness neither lasts nor satisfies the longing for being readmitted to the family. Only within the understanding of sacrificial and substitutionary atonement is true forgiveness powerful.

REPENTANCE

Although not celebrated as a sacrament, repentance is most certainly a sacred act and is therefore sacramental by definition. Further, such action is undoubtedly the most obvious, recognizable result of the ministry of the church. The New Testament book of Acts is a remarkable litany of repentance resulting from lives changed by the gospel. *Webster's Encyclopedic Unabridged Dictionary* defines *repent* as "to turn from sin and dedicate oneself to the amendment of one's life, *a:* to feel regret or contrition, *b:* to change one's mind."[4] The understanding of *repent* within historical Christianity has been "to turn away from," "to forsake" or "to go in a different direction." Without repentance, the results of the gospel would be in vain. It is only with this demonstrable result of preaching that the preacher is able to measure success.

RESTITUTION

Restitution is largely a bygone concept religiously and legally. Within church circles, the word is rarely heard, even though there is strong scriptural admonition for it: "First be reconciled to your brother or sister, and then come and offer your gift" (Mt 5:24). The Old Testament laws in the Pentateuch were strict. Restitution was demanded to promote righteousness within both the avenger and the avenged. Relationships were healed by making things right. There is now a tendency to rationalize wrongdoing and so avoid the consequences. Within the legal system, people are fined and penalized with restitutions that are rarely made. .

Paying back what has been stolen, making right what has been wronged or literally restoring what has been destroyed is a powerful tool toward healing. In the Welsh Revival of 1904–1905, repentance and restitution were integral. W. T. Stead states that "many stories of repentance followed by restitution circulated,"[5] and it is common knowledge in Wales that people were so convicted that they returned tools they had stolen from their employers to the companies' tool sheds. It might be good to reactivate the rite of restitution in the church. After all, action confirms belief.

EUCHARIST

Communion (the Eucharist, which means "thanksgiving") is readily recognized in the church for its sacramental power. Unlike other historical sacraments, baptism and the Lord's Supper have remained essential to all branches of Christendom. While there are differing opinions as to the reification of Communion, there is no debate as to its preeminent value as a powerful healing element. The practice of "gathering around the table" continues to identify those who have been spiritually healed and invites others to the healing that follows forgiveness.

BAPTISM

The sacrament of baptism, which in some assemblies is afforded only to infants and new believers and in other assemblies afforded only to adult believers, is an incredibly powerful and demonstrative tool of faith. It can be argued from a community and psychological point of view that baptism in any form provides a healing framework. It provides the basis, the opportunity and the stage on which individuals, families and congregations can act and reenact relationships, new beginnings and the healing of old hurts. Adult baptism is clearly the announcement of the alignment of the sinner with the Savior and with the family of believers. Infant baptism is a clear demonstration of the acceptance of a new member into the family of God. The innocence of the child permeates and causes all other feelings to be extraneous. Whether it's called baptism or dedication, there is no time equal to that of the birth of a child to affect the brain of its parents. The purpose of discussing baptism in this book is not to debate the method, but to bring attention to the value of this sacrament within the administration of grace—a tool uniquely belonging to the church.

ANOINTING WITH OIL

Many modern congregations have long since given up the practice of anointing with oil. The power of the symbolism of oil along with the individual and intentional attention has profound sacred and very deep interpersonal, psychological meaning. Healing resulting from an anointing is not always the relief of bodily pain or the release from suffering or the delay of death. But it is always a healing experience for those involved, in the deepest spiritual sense.

LAYING ON OF HANDS

The laying on of hands is another practice that has been relegated to a few specific vocations, such as ordination or consecration. The Scriptures are clear about the value of the laying on of hands. Both the Old and the New Testaments mention this practice (see, for example, Num 27:18; Deut 34:9; Mt 19:15; Mk 5:23). Blessings and healing were invoked in a variety of circumstances, although bodily contact in our day and age unfortunately is in disrepute. Simply because there have been occasions of its misuse does not mean that it should be abandoned. The noted Harvard Medical School physician Herbert Benson stated, "I do believe that remembered wellness is at work in therapeutic touch. And additionally, in cases where actual physical contact is made, patients may be benefiting from what I believe will eventually be the scientifically established healing effects of human touch."[6]

It's not difficult to understand the value of human touch, in spite of current taboos on boundary crossing. Anthropological studies have long confirmed the value of human touch. Anthropologist and neurologist André Virel states, "Our skin is a mirror endowed with properties even more wonderful than those of the magic looking glass . . . resulting in a confrontation that stimulates a never-ending movement of images and the birth of what is aptly referred to as reflexive thought."[7]

Skin is the largest organ of the human body and is initiated into human touch at the moment of birth. It is our immediate and lifelong contact with our environment and all that is in it. This dimension of the "other" expels the infant into contact with skin and touch, thus identifying skin with warmth, security and the essentials for survival. It isn't any wonder that the Scriptures speak of "the hand of God" and that Jesus' touch brought healing and life. Further, the touch of Thomas the doubter allowed him to believe in the risen Christ. Touch established belief, and touch revives it.

Anthropologist Ashley Montagu wrote, "Stimulation of the skin apparently constitutes an essential condition in causing the pituitary gland to secrete the hormone most important for the initiation and maintenance of nursing in mammals, including the mother."[8] The significance of this is that touching is a two-way street—it benefits not only the one being touched but also the one doing the touching. The infant's touch of the mother triggers prolactin and oxytocin for milk (colostrum) production in the mother, and the infant's "rooting" for the nipple triggers it to nurse.

The Scriptures are replete with analogies to a loving father and caring mother with comparisons to feeding and touching. We are even enjoined to greet one another with a "holy kiss" (Rom 16:16; 1 Pet 5:14). Therefore, it's important for the ministry of the church, within appropriate and scrupulous boundaries, to reinstitute touch as a ministry of great import. Such touching ought to be considered a sacramental outreach. The common practice of "passing the peace" in many current assemblies is no doubt an attempt to imitate the practice of greeting in the early Christian church.

LAYING ON OF HANDS COUPLED WITH PRAYER

It appears that the laying on of hands coupled with the energies of prayer is especially powerful. The subtle energies (subtle only because we do not understand them) referred to by Tiller in *Subtle Energies, Intentionality and Consciousness* help us to understand the power of prayer, which works when intentionally applied with conscious determination.[9] We are reminded that "the effectual fervent prayer of a righteous man availeth much" (Jas 5:16 KJV).

FOOT WASHING

Few communions continue the practice of foot washing. Some denominations practice foot washing on Maundy Thursday. The scriptural admonition is "If I, your Lord and Teacher, have washed your feet, you also ought to wash one another's feet" (Jn 13:14). Although foot washing was clearly a practice in the New Testament church, the humility of baring our feet and showing our gnarled toes and fungus-infected toenails is less than many want in this day of aesthetic worship. The humility and the recognition of the relationship between the washer and the washed required for foot washing may be a growth process we need to pursue.

PRAYER

Few people would deny the healing power of prayer. We now have scientists of great repute and even religious unbelievers who confess that prayer produces powerful results. The scientific world attempts to discover how prayer works, but they will not find out. It is the energy of God, allowed for human use.

Despite many scientific studies of prayer, none has demonstrated how it works, but most have demonstrated that it does work. Some studies have shown that prayer is effective whether the person being prayed for knows it or not. Larry Dossey, MD, stated, "There have been countless instances in which distant or intercessory prayer succeeds *without the knowledge* of the recipient."[10]

Dossey also recounted an ancient story illustrating the power of prayer: "St. Peregine, while a young priest, . . . was scheduled for amputation of his leg because of a cancer. The night before surgery, he prayed fervently and dreamed he was cured. On awakening his dream had become a reality. He lived to be eighty, dying in 1345 without any further evidence of cancer."[11] Such accounts are legion. Those who wish to do so may attribute them to a hypochondriacal person or to the realm of fantasy; but to those who have experienced it, the power of prayer is a given.

Few scientists disagree that, whatever it is called, there is *energy* at work in prayer that can't be defined. It can't ever be scientifically quantified or defined, since it is one of the mysteries of the spiritual world.

PASTORAL COUNSELING

Counseling, although not considered a sacrament and often not spoken of as a method of ministry, surely is a potential demonstration of grace. The Scriptures are very clear about being in the presence of wise counseling that rests on true wisdom, the wisdom of the Word as authorized by the church. In the past several decades, pastoral counseling has become a specialty for ministers both within and outside the parish. With the development of the professional pastoral counselor, many have tended to diminish the importance of pastoral counseling within the job description of the local minister. This may be a serious mistake, because it tends to secularize this special tool for imparting grace to parishioners. Further, in many circles, professional pastoral counseling has tended to separate itself from the function and ministry of the church per se. Such pastoral counseling may not lose its power as a psychological tool, but risks losing its power as a sacramental tool.

FELLOWSHIP AND FOOD

Other elements within the Christian congregation are distinctively healing, both directly and indirectly. Gathering for fellowship and food is powerful. Although not sacraments, both are opportunities for a profound demonstration of grace. The Scriptures are laden with references to the value of feasting together. There is something about eating with friends that bonds and builds relationships. Breaking bread is sacred and traditionally is done only among friends.

If there has been a breach in the relationship, reconciliation must precede the breaking of bread, hence confession preceding the Eucharist in the Roman Catholic tradition. Christian fellowships would do well to follow this tradition and be reminded in the breaking of bread that it is a celebration of spirituality and a recognition of a healing relationship within the family of God.

Weddings and Funerals

Two of the most prominent demonstrations of grace provided in most congregations, other than worship and the usual church activities, are weddings and funerals (memorials). These ceremonies are not described in the Scriptures, although weddings are referred to (Lk 12:36; 14:8; Jn 2:2). The treatment of the dead is given many more references, particularly preparation for burial (Gen 23:2, 4, 6, 8; 50:26; 1 Sam 15:35; 2 Sam 3:31-34; Eccles 12:5; Jer 7:29). Both weddings and funerals are the recognition of bonding, of the meaning of life, of the purpose of relationships and of God as the essential element in the proclamation of the union of marriage and in the internment of a physical body to the grave and the release of the soul to God.

One function referred to very clearly in the Bible has essentially disappeared from church practice: care of the dead body. Scripture promotes a godly reverence for the body of a dead person, as we see in those who tended to the bodies of Jesus and Lazarus. Though this is not the place for a discussion of the Christian funeral, it's necessary to suggest that recognizing death and the grief process as opportunities for mind-altering ministry may cause reflection on how we care for and bury the dead.

The issue is the opportunity lost when we do not minister to people whose brains, minds and souls are in transition. It's not the wedding ceremony only; it's the preparation, anxiety, expectation and brain in transition that allows for a gate into the soul. Similarly, preparation of the body for burial, which was once the task of the family, is no longer sacred. Respect and care for the "bodily house of a relative" was important, but equally—and perhaps more—important was the preparation by the caregivers as they contemplated their own death and their own eternity. This may be the most important aspect of brain activity in the funeral process. Different parts of the brain are in traumatic transition—struggling against the impulses of anger and fear arising from the amygdala, searching for peace provided by unknown brain physiology (possibly the thalamus) and warding off depression resulting from an imbalance of the neurotransmitter serotonin. Once again, the power of preaching—and, in this case, pastoring—does not rest on transitional physiology; but the minister who understands the process of the transitional brain better can work more easily within a nonjudgmental and empathetic framework.

Capturing the Moment

Weddings and funerals (memorials) are critical "brain times"; they are times when the brain is in flux, when there is psychological trauma. The brain in joy and in grief is open to change and in a state of reflection. The circumstances surrounding death are usually terrifying, confusing and mixed with a myriad of emotions; they force us to face the fragility of life. Often the most primal aspects of our existence are thrust into consciousness. There is nothing like facing mortality to evoke self-reflection. Weddings, deaths and their attendant practices pierce the veil of thinking as usual and challenge the ethos, ethic and ethics of our being. These are prime times when the church and the minister are often welcomed into the innermost cubbyholes of parishioners' lives, and great pastoring can occur. The mind is in a questioning mode.

Times of rejoicing and times of grief are both times when the brain is in transition. There is sound evidence that at such times, the brain is more amenable to new thoughts, new practices and new decisions. These times speak to the core values of our basic philosophies of life. Such opportunities should not be wasted or ignored. When the message of the sermon is not convincing, convicting and decision prompting, the sermon might as well be trashed, because the words likely go to waste; they are only words and have less power than the printed script in a dictionary.

A message and a sermon are not the same; there is a distinctive difference. Messages may be conveyed in a variety of ways: talks, emails, text messages, letters, songs or greeting cards. The sermon is different from any of these or any other method of communication. It's an official method and tool of the church, hopefully Spirit inspired, to convey truth as interpreted by and sanctioned by the church.

The sermon therefore carries authority—actually two authorities: that of the Word itself and that of the denominational or organized body of believers that authorizes the preaching. It must also carry a third authority: that of the minister, who has already been transformed by the sermon. Although God's Word always accomplishes his purposes (Is 55:11), it does not preach itself—the power and purpose of the preacher is essential. "The moment we encounter God, or the idea of God, our brain begins to change."[12] The preached Word cries with power.

Preaching for healing is not necessarily soothing. To be healed, there often must first be surgery or other unpleasant medical procedures. Frequently there are all sorts of medications required in the physical healing process. Some preaching is soothing, but some is surgical. To some, the hearer can say amen, but to others the hearer is left in a state of unrest. Quietude can be a friend of spiritual growth and so can disturbance.

Individuals, families, communities and nations have been torn from each other and from God since Adam and Eve. We may wonder just what argument ensued between Adam and Eve after that first family breach with God and each other. It probably sounded similar to two married partners today in the middle of conflict. The Bible is full of stories of tribes fighting within themselves and among each other. Israel was not only at odds with the Gentile world; brothers betrayed each other. One son faked a hairy body to win an inheritance, and another sold his brother into slavery. Job suffered the torture of bodily pain along with the betrayal of his closest friends. All of these stories and many more testify to our estrangement from one another and from God. They also testify to the healing preached and witnessed throughout the Old Testament.

Nowhere are there more powerful words than in the impassioned power and pathos of Moses' speeches. He and other prophets demonstrate the power of preaching to a disobedient people. Preaching became a central part of Old Testament worship. In the New Testament we see the continued practice of powerful preaching. John the Baptist preached, although to a mocking and unreceptive audience. Jesus taught, performed miracles and preached to throngs, but only a few followed him—and others crucified him.

The great sermon of Peter on the day of Pentecost (Acts 2) demonstrates the power of preaching. Upon hearing the preaching, those who had gathered "were cut to the heart" (v. 37 NIV). Fear (conviction) came upon them, and they "sold their possessions and goods, and parted them to all men as every man had need" (v. 45 KJV). "And they, continuing daily with one accord in the temple, and breaking bread from house to house, did eat their meat with gladness and singleness of heart" (v. 46 KJV). The book of Acts and the entire New Testament is a powerful diary of preachers and the results of powerful preaching. The preaching was for healing—that is, the reconciliation of all creation to God. The pain of separation is still real, and this calls for healing. Preaching speaks to families in disarray, churches in dysfunction and communities in animosity with each other. These conditions may be verbalized as psychological or sociological problems, but they are far more than that. They are illnesses of the souls of those involved, and soul healing rather than community organization is the prescription for regaining health. The sickness is a kind of deep soul sickness. It's a soul sorrow that can't be quieted. Soul sorrow is almost impossible to define, but those who have experienced it do not doubt its reality.

However, preaching has always addressed dysfunction by bringing it out into the open, putting the spotlight of value-laden truth on it and refusing to sweep it under the rug. Soul sorrow is the ache when no apparent relief is in sight. The prophets and preachers of old preached the only relief, and modern ones are encouraged to do the same.

When reading Old Testament stories, it's easy to see the specific conflict or situation to which the preaching spoke. The prophets railed against mistreatment of the poor, disobedience in sacrifices and the evil of the nations. But these great discourses and all other sermon topics are often just that—topics to the listeners. The illness is deeper and much more profound than the greatest oratory could penetrate. It is much more difficult and much more important to see the basic problem underlying all conflict: estrangement from God. This is why powerful, purposeful preaching is needed; it offers a gift to the world that only the church through its preaching can give.

The New Testament carries forward the same dynamic initiated by the prophets. John the Baptist introduced Jesus in a demanding, prophetic and indeed dramatic fashion. Jesus preached the kingdom, telling about the man blind from birth, the woman with many husbands and the brother raised from the dead. But these, and all other accounts described in the Scriptures, are not the reason for the preaching. Paul continued the divine order of preaching in his missionary journeys, and, like the prophets and Jesus, he suffered persecution from unbelievers.

The miracles and parables of Jesus and the sermons and workings of the disciples and apostles are illustrations from life that demanded attention to *the reason for preaching*. The reason is basic. It is foundational to all that is in the Holy Writ. The reason is the basic conflict, the basic separation, the basic illness and the basic breach of a relationship between God and his creation.

"The preacher is in a very distinct sense a trustee. . . . Those who have accepted the responsibility imposed on them by this Divine commission are enjoined to exercise their office so as to warrant the approbation of Him who has appointed them to a specific work."[13] Luther is quoted as having said, "The devil does not mind the written word, but he is put to flight whenever it is preached aloud."[14]

Much preaching is misunderstood (inadequately powerful) and misdirected (insufficiently purposeful). Many fail to see the *reason* behind the sermon—sometimes even the preacher. The specific purpose for that specific sermon may not be clear. Each sermon must be *intentionally directed toward a specific purpose*. When this is the case, everyone gains and prepares for the next installment. Can you imagine church members waiting in anticipation for the next sermon?

Both immediate and long-term results can be expected from purposeful preaching. Immediate results are the accumulation of accepted and integrated previous learning. Results are both long-term and immediate when integrated into what a person knows will be needed or does not yet know due to immaturity or ignorance. Even before birth, the brain starts learning what it will eventually need to know and stores information for future use. "Long-term memory requires the synthesis of new proteins and the growth of new synaptic connections. With repetition of a specific stimulus, the synthesis and activation of proteins alter the neuron's excitability and promote the growth of new synaptic connections."[15] We learn through consistent, repetitious teaching—whether it is mathematics or theology. On the immediate the long term is built, and on the long term the immediate happens.

Most sermons are measured only by immediate results. The preacher preaches without focus, and devoted followers predictably comply by giving unfocused attention and varying responses. Preachers look for the *results*: new members, more contributions and more converts. Those results are never the real result, but the *result of the basic result*. The basic result is found in a realignment of relationship, from which all other results follow. The realignment of relationship begins with a realignment of self and God, then self and others, and then others and the world in which we live. Preaching only for immediate results is like attempting to paint a house that hasn't been built.

Modern theology and modern medicine suffer a similar malady. Both often work at symptom relief without attending to the basic cause of the illness. Relieving a headache may feel good temporarily, but if the basic cause of the pain isn't addressed, a person may die of a brain tumor while enjoying symptom relief. In the church, we have sermons that mollify emotional pain, sugarcoat conflict and label deviances from God's way as "individual differences." But renaming something does not change what it is.

Illness is separation from health. Possessing health is much more than not being sick. *Health is the homeostasis of mind, body and spirit within divine relationship to God.* This is true whether we are speaking of emotional illness, physical illness, interpersonal conflict, domestic upset, tribal skirmishes or nations at war.

Purposeful preaching both diagnoses and treats. Often the diagnosis is too narrow, too limited, such as identifying a singular sin. But there is no such thing as a singular sin. Sins are like stacked dominoes; no one domino falls alone. Further, sin can't be undone—

it can only be forgiven. Deviation from God's intended harmony produces cataclysmic waves beyond anything that can be seen. All of life is within relationship. Nothing occurs in isolation or without reverberations. Acts of disobedience to God produce waves like a pebble, whose ripples are ongoing.

This is where preaching comes in. It addresses the larger picture, which is the deepest picture—the reconciliation of the whole of creation. This is the foundation of all relationships and all healing. Believers have been given this awesome responsibility:

> All this is from God, who reconciled us to himself through Christ and gave us the ministry of reconciliation: that God was reconciling the world to himself in Christ, not counting people's sins against them. And he has committed to us the message of reconciliation. We are therefore Christ's ambassadors, as though God were making his appeal through us. We implore you on Christ's behalf: Be reconciled to God. God made him who had no sin to be sin for us, so that in him we might become the righteousness of God. (2 Cor 5:18-21 NIV)

The original idea of healing arose out of the Old Testament concept of holiness, which spoke of an intimate, personal and *total* relationship to God the Holy One. In more recent times, the concept of *totalness* or *completeness* has been diminished to body and mind healing or wholeness.

The Hebrew term *qādôš* is expressed in the Greek words *hagios* and *holoklēria* and several other derivations of those words, all having to do with a totality of healing. Becoming holy is much more than getting religion. It is also far more than retaining or regaining body/mind health. This Old Testament theme continues in the New Testament. Both the Greek and the Hebrew words for "holy" indicate wholeness. To speak only of body/mind healing is to be earthbound, or terrestrially hedonistic, and temporary in the broadest sense of that word.

Paul used the adjective *holoklēros*, which speaks to the same concept of completeness—that is, total relationship to the Holy One. "Now may the Lord of peace himself give you peace at all times in all ways [*holoklēron*]" (2 Thess 3:16). *Holoklēria* is the noun form of *holoklēron,* which carries both the Hebrew and the Greek concept of wholeness into the English vocabulary.

When speaking of *holoklēros,* we must use *term* rather than *word,* because the verb and noun of that bit of grammar are far more than single words. They refer to a concept, a philosophy that underlies the basis of all preaching and, for that matter, all life. Nothing is holy in and of itself, including the redeemed human. Holiness comes only by being totally and unconditionally consecrated and *bound* within the relationship to the Almighty; holiness can never be complete in human earthly form. From these words we have derived many similar words, such as *healing, health, holiness* and *wholeness.* These refer to a completeness in which the body, mind, soul, relationships and the creation itself surrender to reconciliation with their Creator. Preaching must address the *completeness* of salvation—that is, the reunification of souls, bodies, minds and relationships to God. These words establish the biblical philosophical base on which everything that fits together in the unity of God is built.

The difficulty is that the words translate easily etymologically, but no longer communicate the original concept of an unblemished, uninterrupted, intimate, continuous and inextricably interwoven relationship to the Holy One. We have lost the concept of the creation in unity with God; this includes all that was created—earth, sea, skies and all they contain. This unity has been ignored by most mainline theology and relegated to polytheism. Nothing could be further from the truth.

Philosophies, such as our folkways and mores, are woven into the very warp and woof of a culture and continuously eclipse actions of the Godhead. It's hard to find the Holy One in the midst of a materialistic, hedonistic, terrestrial philosophy. Theology, like all philosophies, has been influenced by every culture. Those who go to church for the preaching and those who do the preaching are influenced and largely controlled in all of daily life by a culture of the unholy, except perhaps for those few minutes of preaching. Although the so-called unholy aspects of life may be defined as secular, in truth, all of life is sacred. Therefore, what we perceive as the unholy is actually a perversion of the sacred. Christians are set apart as holy agents for the purpose of glorifying God; therefore, all that we do, think and say is intended to be holy.

To think of some things as secular and other things as sacred allows for a false sense of being and an erroneous concept of belonging to God. But our experience is further manifestation of our inability to secularize even the most sacred. With all of the attempts of the media and postmodern technology, the sacred still stands out and can't be hidden. God is present, whether recognized or not.

Since we are redeemed sinners, we are in a constant state of being made holy. *Holoklēria* suggests the *process* of being made permanently healthy *in all parts*—that is, restored in relationship to God in soul, mind, body and community. This process is similar to that spoken of by Paul: "And I am convinced *and* sure of this very thing, that He Who began a good work in you will continue until the day of Jesus Christ [right up to the time of His return], developing [that good work] *and* perfecting *and* bringing it to full completion in you" (Phil 1:6 Amplified Bible).

Expounded in this verse is the truth that "man can't complete his own life. . . . Over against all secularism, which puts man's salvation in his own hands, there stands the inescapable fact that neither the beginning nor the end of anything is in our hands."[16]

The entire earth, including humans, constantly yearns for completeness (*holoklēria*). The spiritual mind understands that such completeness is not available except through grace given to us, not as a hedonistic possession but rather as an instrument for unification with God and with the creation that surrounds us, including "heaven and earth, the sea, and all that is in them" (Ps 146:6).

Preaching, therefore, can't be piecemeal. Preaching as if there are parts to be addressed misses the concept of God's wholeness. It is the whole or nothing at all. In truth, it is all or nothing.

Much has been made of the erroneous Cartesian separation of mind and body, and correctly so. However, insufficient attention has been given to the separation of the other elements in a broken world. To see the mind and the body as separate is no longer a reasonable choice. Any such conceived separation is purely imaginary, which has been more than adequately proven by neuroscience, a plethora of research and voluminous clinical studies. If we could scan interpersonal and international conflict relationships as we do the human body, we would see the same thing. There can be no breach between any part of God's creation without causing fundamental illness of every part involved. Powerful, productive preaching addresses this basic illness. Illnesses of all sorts began with a basic separation from God, and health can't be reclaimed until the breach is healed.

Preaching and the Brain in Pain

We know that the whole creation groaneth and
travaileth in pain together until now.

PAUL (ROM 8:22 KJV)

Recent medical technologies, such as scans and MRIs, have shown with scientific accuracy how the brain responds favorably to information that offers hope, peace and tranquility. Electroencephalogram records have shown brain-wave amplitude and type changing with various verbal inputs, such as preaching styles.

The problem of pain is as old as civilization and as unfathomable now as it was to Job. Everyone experiences pain, and no one likes it. To some people, pain has religious meaning; for example, it might be seen as the result of having sinned or as necessary for soul growth. For most people, pain is worth the agony to stay alive, even if the pain is acute and medication doesn't alleviate it.

The purpose of this discussion is not to revisit the age-old question of why there is pain in the world, but rather to look at ways that preaching can positively affect the experience of pain. In practical terms, preaching may have a greater influence on suffering than on pain, but rarely are these two terms separable. Few people are able to tell exactly where pain leaves off and suffering begins.

The preacher shouldn't abdicate the attempt to alleviate actual physical and mental pain as well as the accompanying suffering. Knowledge of how the brain works dramatically improves a pastor's ability in this area. Music, Scripture readings, prayer, the sacraments, the minister's physical presence and many other factors actually reduce pain. Again, this has been proven scientifically.

Although pain is certainly more than mere perception, by putting our experiences in proper perspective, the experience of pain is altered—and frequently the pain is lessened.[1]

The brain itself—that is the actual brain tissue—does not feel pain; it interprets pain. Therefore pain is interpreted within the context and culture as well as the psychobiological memories of past experiences. This often adds the potential for secondary gain, that is, the benefits of pain. Some people seem to actually gain benefits from pain ranging from compensation to various degrees of martyrdom. Some see pain as a potential resolution of karma, a method for manipulation of employers and family, or an approach to controlling organizations by avoiding regulations and other expectations of those not in pain. Pain in and of itself is not necessarily emotionally unhealthy, but the uses and abuses of it are often manifestations of psychological disturbances.

Pain must not be seen as an enemy. Without pain, we could die without knowing we were sick. Pain is a friend. However, pain may become sufficiently prolonged and intense that it no longer serves as a warning device but becomes an illness itself. This is often the case in degenerative and terminal illnesses. Only recently has the medical profession designated pain as an illness. For the most of human history, pain has been considered by much of the religious world as having to do with some kind of karma or repayment for disobedience or violations of God's standards.

These and many other interpretations become the basis for purposeful preaching as it relates to pain. Apart from God's healing, preaching itself is certainly not credited as relieving pain. But that may be a mistake, because preaching can relieve pain. Remember, the spoken word becomes the basis for neurobiological functioning. Increasingly neurotechnology is showing how body parts, even prosthetic appendages, can be controlled by thought alone. The mind has always been capable of such powers, but only now in the age of neuroscientific measurement can we definitively show a cause/effect relationship. Experimenters are showing how to turn neurons on and off by thought processes. Psychologists, psychiatrists and others trained in the art of hypnosis have been demonstrating such for centuries but without the benefit of the now available scientific validation. Wireless neurotransmitters, utilizing brain signals, have shown the ability to control neurotransmitters that in turn determine our behavior.[2] Further, the mind has shown the ability to work directly upon behavioral patterns as a result of persuasion, which again we already knew but were unable to measure as we now can.[3] Beth Azar notes, "Our data are consistent with the notion that if you can get someone to step into your shoes psychologically, you might be halfway home in terms of persuading them to see the content of the message the way you want them to."[4] In the light of this kind of information, why and how can we doubt the power of purposeful preaching?

Preaching for healing recognizes that pain and suffering are different. Some have pain but little or no suffering, while others have suffering with little or no pain. Suffering is an emotional concept that comes from an individual's understanding of life. It often has meaning deeply rooted in family systems, cultural backgrounds and religious beliefs. Although preaching may at times relieve actual physical pain, that's not its primary purpose. However, preaching should help to bring meaning and clarification to suffering.

The preacher is a prime mover in changing the meaning of pain and suffering. The process of neuroplasticity is involved in such understanding. "Understanding" is often a matter of the brain changing its neurological connections—that is, rearranging its "switchboard."

Examples within the faith process are such things as watching the formation of faith (thought processes) become activated faith, which produces changes in behavior (new neurological patterns and reflexes). In many ways, preaching coaxes the brain into change. Faith can't be forced, but rather is enticed as a result of rethinking (cognition change) to positive reward recognition as a result of behavioral reconstruction.

People who are able to transcend the physical and find meaning in the spiritual are often able to reduce both pain and suffering. Suffering is reduced when we see a reason for it or understand that we have power over it, even if we are unable to alleviate the pain medically.

Readers of the Scriptures are sometimes caught up in the magnificent and wonderful healings of Jesus, while not understanding that they are primarily illustrations of God's power. Healings were performed that people might believe. Producing belief and faith has always been the purpose for preaching and belief, and faith continues to be the basis for healing.

Brain Healing and the Soul

He satisfieth the longing soul, and filleth the hungry soul with goodness.

PSALM 107:9 KJV

Soul pain is real. Numerous respected medical and psychological experts attest to the fact that when the brain is in turmoil, the body does not heal as well. And when the soul (even for those who reject the idea of a soul) finds healing—some call it forgiveness or catharsis—the body and mind work together to heal each other.

The soul and its relationship to God has largely been considered mythical and imaginary by the scientific community—*until now*. Recent studies clearly show a relationship between health and illness greater than what can be explained by anatomy, physiology, neurochemistry or any other science. Belief is now considered neurobiologically significant and has specific pertinence to preaching.

Cell biologist Bruce Lipton stated, "We are one with a bigger universe/God."[1] In not too distant ages, scientists were persecuted, and some lost their lives for proclaiming a scientific view. "Science eventually displaced the Church as civilization's source of wisdom for understanding the mysteries of the universe."[2] It is possible that the tide is turning. Our knowledge of the human body and its functions is now so vast that we understand the intricacies of a cellular and neurobiological nature, which demands that we believe in more than physiology.

Neuroscientists are finding functions in the brain that point to spiritual thinking, honesty and other values consistent with a Christian philosophy. These values can't be accounted for by the three primary elements of human existence: chemistry, neuroelectricity and anatomy. Nor can they be accounted for by discovering more about neurological locations of human emotion. The concept of soul has survived in spite of philosophers, scientists and skeptics for thousands of years, and it is alive and well today.

The sciences have attempted to reduce the human being to physical anatomy. This reductionist approach doesn't explain the complexities of human behavior. During the past century, psychologists and biologists worked intensely at moving toward finding the physical reasons for human behavior, but they have been famously unsuccessful. Modern psychiatry is a perfect illustration of the scientific attempt to reduce human behavior to neuroanatomy, neurochemicals and neuropharmacology. Most psychiatrists have abandoned psychotherapy in favor of the organic (that is, psychopharmacological) approach. While doubtless there are many medically correct indications for chemical intervention, most psychiatrists concede that neuropharmacy mostly addresses symptoms, not causes. When fully effective, medicines allow the body to heal itself.

There is still no absolute proof of the supremacy of thought over brain chemistry or brain chemistry over thought. It has been abundantly demonstrated that in many instances psychotherapy has proven to be as effective in altering brain chemistry as pharmacotherapy. The "chicken and egg" argument will not be solved until we recognize that neither the brain nor the body is able to act alone, but only in tandem.

Further, the concept of soul is unequivocal theologically. St. Thomas Aquinas said, "God can't make a man to have no soul."[3]

To the contrary, scientist and author Carl Sagan said, "My fundamental premise about the brain is that its workings—what we sometimes call 'mind'—are a consequence of its anatomy and physiology and nothing more."[4] This thinking is typical of many scientific minds, but such reductionism dismisses the concept of soul and further reduces the mind to a process based solely on what can be scientifically demonstrated. Since a brain can be seen, dissected and studied objectively, this allows some to dismiss the idea of "mind," since it can't be subjected to the same processes. Within the spiritual realm, we aren't limited to what can be seen and handled. Reality is more than our physical capabilities can encounter, envision and define. Although much of human behavior can now be attributed to specific brain chemistry, anatomical brain functioning and alterations in brain electricity, nothing apart from God has been able to explain the mystical part of the human.

Clergy are acquainted with dealing with another concept altogether—faith, which bridges science to real life and translates what can't be proved to the pragmatic. Admitting to the reality of the soul is not magic. Magic is sleight of hand, deception. Faith is mystical, not magical; it is believing in unseen realities: "Now faith is the substance of things hoped for, the evidence of things not seen" (Heb 11:1 KJV). From a Christian perspective, faith is not speculative; it is the *substance* (physical matter), the objective and subjective recognition of the *evidence* (proof of) an actual material presence.

It's amazing that someone can write an entire book that is otherwise remarkably valuable without having the words *God* or *theology* in the index. Such is the case with *The Seat of the Soul* by Gary Zukav. Its assumption, although not stated, is that when speaking of value-laden humanness, we are speaking of God. Such philosophy is devoid of an understanding of anything other than the material world and is in denial of what perpetuates the constant search for meaning by the human race in all ages.[5]

In a vain attempt to deny God as part of the unanswerable, the word *spirituality* has become fashionable. It is now completely proper to discuss spirituality but not religion, even within medical and other scientific venues, where it was taboo just a few years ago. Professionals were prohibited from discussing spirituality with clients and patients, for fear of ethical recrimination. Today there are whole schools of thought springing up utilizing a spiritual base. Martin Seligman's Positive Psychology (in which academic degrees are granted at the University of Pennsylvania in the Positive Psychology program) is based on the positive mental attitude that has been preached by theologians and motivational speakers for centuries (to name a few, Norman Vincent Peale, Harry Emerson Fosdick, Dale Carnegie and Cardinal Fulton J. Sheen). These and many other "new theories" of how the mind regains and retains mental health are only as new as the book of Proverbs in the Bible and the recorded wisdom of other ancients. They are based on the assumption of mental abilities beyond what human physiology can explain—namely, a power within—the soul.

The preacher must preach to the soul. But how is this done? Since the spoken word calls for the attention of the brain and listening demands the attention of the mind, we must look to the more amorphous and ethereal abilities of the human. These are found in symbols, rituals and liturgy. Many communities of Christians have abandoned traditional church symbolism, believing them to be pagan. However, such symbols did not derive from paganism, but from within the practices of the Judeo-Christian faith. Reasons for retaining or abandoning liturgy, rituals and symbols have often been tied to denominational, pseudotheological and faulty philosophy rather than to solid church history or theology.

If you were to ask most Protestants why they don't observe certain sacraments, the answer would be, "Because Presbyterians [or another group of Protestants] don't do that." Conversely, if you were to ask some Roman Catholics why they observe certain sacraments, they would say, "Because that's what Catholics do." There must be better reasons for us to maintain or abandon practices than simply because of tradition.

Modernizing is nothing new. The church has both maintained its historical roots and morphed for centuries and will doubtlessly continue to do so. However, as with any institution that changes, care must be taken to produce a product that is *needed* as well as *wanted*. Eventually need outlives want.

Believers need vigorous reasons for what they affirm. We are admonished by the apostle Peter, "Always be ready to make your defense to anyone who demands from you an accounting for the hope that is in you; yet do it with gentleness and reverence" (1 Pet 3:15-16). From the brain-functioning point of view, concrete actions such as baptism, the Eucharist and confession stimulate memory-enhancing neural pathways. Those who decry such sacraments often do so with what they label as theological belief. But in most assemblies, other actions are made sacramental by pronouncement, denominational doctrine or habitual practice.

As has been seen previously in this book, the brain needs repetition, simplicity and consistency to create neural pathways capable of changing thought and behavior. And what else is the church about, if it isn't that?

The brain learns and stores memory in various compartments. It appears from the most recent research that the brain identifies stimuli in many different ways and places the memories of those stimuli in various brain locations that respond to several different methods of retrieval. For instance, experiences in which we are personally and physically involved tend to be stored in visual memory banks. As a result, when that memory is recalled, it is accompanied with an image of what the eye saw. Memories of reading material, for example, tend to be recalled without visual imagery (except by those who have what is called a photographic memory).

Both kinds of memory, and other kinds of stored memory,

remain stable for only short periods and very quickly adapt due to preexisting memory patterns and superimposed new data. Three people viewing an incident report the incident differently not only because of initial input but also because of previously engrammed data that is more consistent with the new information. Each of the three then gives a very different story from her or his first story after a few hours. This is because it is a one-time-stimulus input. As has been stated, repetition of the same stimuli tends to offer the best basis for stable long-term memory.

Since every item learned has a specific use and a specific time allocation for its use, the learned information morphs over time and must be relearned within new contexts continuously. This is where repetitively consistent information (such as nonambiguous preaching) comes into neuroscientific application. It's also where various kinds of learning—such as symbolic, verbal, intuitional and imagery—are blended into meaning.

Symbols are not simply objectifications of artistic thoughts. They convey overt and covert messages that can't be verbalized. "Symbols speak . . . as words do not. Symbols allow for individual interpretation, and [with] rituals invite and enable the larger community into a common belief and celebration of that belief."[6] Langer pointed out that we can't live without symbols.[7] In fact, symbols announce the meaning of words, rather than words defining symbols.

> Symbols and rituals work together in most of life. This combination is particularly important since the church utilizes both on a regular basis. Symbols and rituals make adaptation, coping, and translation possible on an individual level while communicating with a larger community. They permit information to be revisited within the context of new information, and likewise permit it to become integrated into old information which is already in place.[8]

Symbols serve as neuropsychological bridges that span time, relationships and circumstances in a way that words can't, whether they are read or heard.

Many symbols were born out of necessity to preserve the physical lives of believers, such as the ichthus (sign of the fish), which was used by early Christians to identify themselves with other believers during times of persecution. The sign of the fish arose on the fishing shores of that era—very appropriate identifiers for a seafaring society. During the years from A.D. 54 to 307 (when Constantine became emperor), this symbol saved the lives of many believers.

Since the Reformation, gesturing the sign of the cross has largely been discarded by Protestants. The *Signum Crucis* has deep roots, however, and need not be considered Roman Catholic or Orthodox. Martin Luther, the notable reformer, did not abandon the sign of the cross, but blessed and used it. In Roman Catholicism, this symbolism signifies the Holy Trinity and the five wounds of Christ (the five fingers on the hand making the sign). In many instances, the sign of the cross is abandoned not out of knowledge, but simply because it is presumed to be Catholic. However, most people can't tell you the origin or meaning of the practice or why they do or don't observe it.

The loss of symbols and rituals is critical. They are major brain gates. Symbols speak to the soul. Worship services in the early church were built on symbols and rituals. Many Protestant churches pride themselves on the lack of symbolism and ritual in their services, particularly the more conservative ones. New sanctuaries are built with little attention to symbols. It's unfortunate that some megachurches require careful inspection to find any signs that they are churches.

There are many other symbols, far too many to mention here. However, simply because a denomination or church does not use the traditional symbols does not mean that it is symbol-free. It simply develops its own without calling them symbols. So why not use the tried and proven rather than making worshipers guess?

Symbols allow for individual interpretation, and rituals invite the larger community into a common belief and celebration of that belief. Concretizing the abstract is essential to learning. Learning can't be separated from faith. To learn, we must have faith in what is being taught. We can learn from a teacher we don't like, don't agree with and don't trust. But to retain knowledge, we must believe that what is being taught has value. The value is always wrapped up in the meaning of the symbols or rituals of that learning. For instance, we learn certain information in college to pass an exam, which is the ritual. We learn by association, by building new knowledge on old. The old knowledge can serve as symbols to which we can attach new meaning. Everything we learn is founded and expressed in symbols, and those symbols can be, and usually are, tied together in rituals.

All language is comprised of symbols. There is a myriad of other symbols that speak to us, such as traffic lights, the cross on a steeple and the flag on the post office. Nearly every thought and action in life is symbol based. Symbols cross all language barriers. For example, a picture of a pedestrian or a cigarette with a mark through it conveys words without using them.

Wedding rings, flowers, organ music, wedding attire and much more are present in a wedding, but only together do they form a ritual called a wedding. Otherwise they're elements of the ritual but not the ritual itself. Here is the secret of the brain's organization: it arranges symbols into already known and accepted environmental, cultural and previously learned pathways to form meaning. When previous experiences have prepared the brain in other than culturally accepted ways, dysfunction occurs—but the dysfunction may not be understood or even noticed by the one experiencing it. What seems deviant and wrong to others appears to be appropriate and right to the previously ill-prepared brain.

It isn't possible to overemphasize the role of brain preparation early in life. The mother's disposition, the father's treatment, the family's acceptance and even the words heard from before birth become the symbols and foundation for all thought and action that will follow throughout life. The infant may not appear to be hearing, but the words put into that little brain early on are heard in ways we don't understand. We know that babies can differentiate between a smiling face and a scowling face and respond accordingly. Words are not necessary for communication; symbols exist in many other forms.

Without symbols, there is a paucity of meaning, and without rituals, there is a loss of community. Therefore, maintaining clear understanding of symbols and rituals is critical to teaching faith. They allow learning to occur within an accepted framework, and they build on symbolic and ritualistic knowledge already assimilated into our belief system. Long before we knew what we were learning, our parents, siblings and society deeply instilled within us the symbols by which we learn more fully all that we will ever know.

Harvey Cox, a Harvard theologian, writes of recalling pictures of biblical scenes on the walls of his childhood Sunday school classroom, the music about those pictures and how they wore bathrobes and other things to act out the scenes. "By the time we were ready to leave Sunday school, these sagas had become permanent features in the topography of our imagination. They did exactly what rituals are supposed to do."[9]

Symbols and rituals can provide a process by which we gain insight and understanding of both present and past relationships. They promote a process by which we can reconstruct and repair breaches in both present and past relationships. They provide meaning to myth, allowing us to maintain a healthy, whole person within ourselves, our communities and our families. Thus they can provide an individual process that brings emotional healing, regardless of the wishes or participation of others.

How do symbols and rituals work, and why are they essential to worship? Symbols and rituals become the basis for already accepted beliefs and provide a trusted base on which to receive new knowledge. Even new information that we doubt can be accepted if it fits into a gestalt already in place. Symbols and rituals make adaptation, coping and translation possible on an individual level while communicating with a larger community. They permit us to revisit old information within the context of new information and, likewise, permit us to integrate new information into old information already in place. Symbols and rituals allow us to identify with a value base without having to put it into new words. In fact, symbols and rituals *force* us to identify what we *can't* put into words. For example, prayer is clearly a ritual that, as the Scriptures state, allow us to talk with God with "groans that words cannot express" (Rom 8:26 NIV 1984).

Symbols and rituals discourage argumentation because we so completely accept them, and we know that others have their own interpretation as well. They announce that the meaning of words and actions emanates from the inner person and so are egosyntonic, meaning that they fit with our innermost person—our soul. They don't readily permit technical analysis, and they escape the scientific method. Their true meaning is entirely too personal to be analyzed by anyone else, and we can't easily analyze them ourselves.

The meaning of symbols is far more emotional than intellectual; therefore, to revisit information built on these already accepted symbols and rituals, the veil of emotion must be penetrated. Penetrating the tough psychological membrane that sheaths our already accepted beliefs isn't easy. People who voice little faith in the United States, for instance, can get very concerned when someone threatens to burn the American flag. Even those who never attend church may tell you that they are comforted by the steeple with a cross on top. Certain community symbols carry more emotional investment than others. For example, the act of torching a church out of violence usually has much more meaning, even to non-churchgoers, than torching a corner store.

Symbols have meaning, very deep meaning, the depth of which isn't always known until the destruction of that symbol is threatened. Rituals also have deep meaning. The entire ritual is threatened when one or more symbols within that ritual are threatened. Again, the wedding ring (symbol) does not make a wedding (ritual). However, when the wedding ring is taken off after a divorce, the ritual of the previous wedding ceremony takes on a very different meaning.

As mentioned earlier, Langer pointed out in her *Philosophy in a New Key* that we can't live without symbols. She helps us to understand that signs and symbols are two different things.[10] I stated in my book *The Sacrament of Psychology,*

> A symbol means to each person something very unique and no one can tell another person exactly what that is. A sign, on the other hand, may be interpreted by everyone as meaning the same thing. Other signs however, are both universally accepted and yet have highly personalized interpretations. The sign of the cross, a fish, a Star of David, a wedding band, a nation's flag, etc., while having broad general interpretation, can have highly individualized and specific meanings to each individual. However, signs (which are ritualized symbols), speak the same message to all.[11]

An illustration of such a symbol is the stop sign, which becomes a ritual observed by all motorists the same way.

We find our individual reality and purposes in our own unique symbols. We live by symbols, and it's not difficult to find each individual's unique and meaningful symbols. Therapists who understand symbols and rituals have found them to be valuable in therapeutic interventions. We find that symbols range from a keepsake to a watch given by a relative to a picture on the wall to items we might never expect to have meaning. For example, after the September 2, 1998, Swissair Flight 111 airplane disaster over Halifax, Nova Scotia, CNN showed pictures of Red Cross workers collecting stones from the shoreline as mementos for mourning relatives.

Once again, we ask why the church and its preachers should discard valuable tools in the preaching of the Word. Is it time to revisit practices that have endured because "that's the way we have always done it"?

Refusing to utilize symbols, watering down rituals and denying the power of liturgy doesn't rob those functions of power; it simply robs worshipers of it. Finally, the scientific world has come to recognize that there is something more to the human being than flesh and bones. And if we are to move forward scientifically or otherwise, that "something more" must be recognized and no longer denied. They are talking about the soul. You would think that preachers would welcome this new knowledge and wonder why it took theologians so long to catch up.

Caring for the soul is probably the most intense, internally felt aspect of a pastor's experience. It requires personal soul searching and soul care to find the inner strength and integrity to be authentic. Ministers who would guide others must surely find ways to know themselves first. With some exceptions, this rarely occurs. Psychologists and psychiatrists who guide others must surely find the Spirit and the source of that energy within themselves first, as do ministers. While some ministers have not pursued knowing themselves, many psychologists and psychiatrists certainly have not looked for the Spirit or the source of their energy.

Those who wish to help others must be able to transcend not only themselves but also the words and actions of their disciplines. The method is not the message. Neither can the message be reduced to the method. The message is inseparably and inextricably interwoven with transcendence. Transcendence is a *spiritual* ability to pervade, translate, communicate and exceed all messages and all methods. "Transcendence is to rise above, go beyond, and to experience more than the here-and-now could predict or anticipate."[12]

Ministers, psychologists, psychiatrists, physicians of all sorts and all who are healers in any profession must allow God to bring about transcendence beyond our frail human selves so we can rely on a spiritual depth and energy beyond our knowledge and definition.

When floundering, pastors accept an amorphous, ever-changing social philosophy to replace their theology—and it doesn't work. Parishioners don't expect social work or psychotherapy from the pastor; they expect and should receive theologically, biblically based pastoral care. Patients in soul pain quickly see the difference between environmental, social and psychological manipulation and the "peace of God, which surpasses all understanding" (Phil 4:7).

Even the most successful mind manipulation doesn't last in the face of new trauma, and soul trauma tends to continue long after the immediate cause has dissipated. Deep within the human person is a longing for wholeness—holiness, godliness, soul health. The emotion of the moment may be dealt with by mental manipulation, but the soul yearns for truth that transcends daily problems. Both neuroscience and theology agree that to bring about a long-lasting result, the very core of the person must be changed.

Christians agree that those who believe in Christ are new creatures; indeed, their very core has changed: "So if anyone is in Christ, there is a new creation: everything old has passed away; see, everything has become new!" (2 Cor 5:17). Those who preach to symptom relief rather than to total Christocentric transformation come to recognize that their primary tools are only pacifiers and that unless the basic spiritual problem is dealt with, only pacification is the result. The cry can be subdued, but not the pain.

Brain Healing and the Mind

*For God hath not given us the spirit of fear; but of power,
and of love, and of a sound mind.*

PAUL (2 TIM 1:7 KJV)

The brain (the way we think) changes the way we act. It is part of the physical anatomy of the body, and the mind is the soul that carries out the thinking of the brain. When the brain is sick, so are actions. If we are to change people's actions, we must first heal the brain. New science tells us about neuroplasticity—the ability of the brain to rewire itself and thus restore the mind.

The mind is distinct from soul and spirit. When speaking of healing the mind, immediately the concept of retaining or regaining mental health enters the picture. Certainly healing the mind includes maintaining mental health and eliminating diseases of the mind. However, healing the mind is much more. In fact, dealing with mental illness, when thought of from a psychological point of view, is perhaps the least of its meanings.

The dictionary definition of *mind* is "that which perceives, feels, wills, etc."[1] An even better definition in relation to preaching is that of Corsini: "The organized totality of mental and psychic processes of an organism, and the structural and functional components upon which they depend."[2] Preaching to heal the mind is then helping others to think clearly, reason accurately and use good judgment.

The apostle Paul said, "Let the same mind be in you that was in Christ Jesus" (Phil 2:5). Understanding this verse helps with preaching to heal the mind. We can start by asking the obvious questions: Why do we think as we do? What do we think is important? Do we consciously try to think in a Christian way? Does our thinking soundly reflect New Testament teaching?

There are three very important words in that verse: *mind, be* and *Jesus.* It's imperative to understand the word *be,* which is used both as a verb and a noun. The verb is in gerund form (*ing*)—*being*—which refers to a process. The noun form refers to *location.* Therefore, when exhorted to let "this mind be," we understand that the mind of Christ has both *location* and *process.* Preaching describes that location and that process. Preaching provides the platform for instructing believers in both aspects of allowing the mind of Christ to be in our lives.

Both the Greek and the Hebrew words rendered as *mind* are ambiguous when translated, since both cultures utilized several words attempting to convey the meaning. If our modern knowledge of neuroscience had been available at that time, the translation may have been more exact. The Greek terms *nous, dianoia* and *synesis* are the most prevalent words used in the New Testament. The Old Testament word most commonly used is *lēb,* which means "that of an intellectual and emotional nature."[3] Each conveys a slightly different meaning, but all have the same ultimate interpretation: "enlightened from above."[4] Preaching could have no greater gift than to be the instrument by which heavenly enlightenment might occur. It's clear that mind and memory are tandem and physiologically similar if not identical. The mind can work only from a foundation of memory, and memory can only work with the integration of brain matter and function that is called "mind." Some might argue about which precedes the other, but for our purposes, it doesn't matter. The concepts of mind and memory are essential elements for successful preaching and are imperative, basic principles of this book.

The power of the mind is still greatly underestimated, even by neuroscientists. Meditation and prayer are functions of the mind that we have all experienced. What we have also experienced, but may be much less aware of, is the power that such practices have on our lives. It was reported in the last few years that "neuroscientists at the Mayo Clinic campus in Jacksonville, Fla., have demonstrated how brain waves can be used to type alphanumerical characters on a computer screen. By merely focusing on the 'q' in a matrix of letters, for example, that 'q' appears on the monitor."[5] This kind of mind-machine interface is staggering, and the potential for us to appreciate the power of prayer further is phenomenal. It gives us a whole new understanding of what is meant by having the mind of Christ.

This knowledge should cause Christians to consider seriously what Jesus meant when—after healing the sick, giving sight to the blind and raising the dead—he said, "I assure you, most solemnly I tell you, if anyone steadfastly believes in Me, he will himself be able to do the things that I do; and he will do even greater things than these, because I go to the Father" (Jn 14:12 Amplified Bible).

Many commentaries interpret Philippians 2:5-8 as exhorting us to imitate Christ's humility. And certainly that message is clear. But humility is only a part of the mind of Christ. The greater part is thought processes, belief abilities, levels of trust and obedience to God's plan. Christ's humility did not start with deciding to be humble. Humanly speaking, it began with the thinking process that accepted the Father's plan for his life, even with the knowledge that such a plan would include pain and suffering.

A Carmelite monk named Nicolas Herman, known to the Christian world as Brother Lawrence (1614–1691), wrote *The*

Practice of the Presence of God. This book became (and remains) popular among Roman Catholics and Protestants alike, due to its clear understanding of living the "mind of Christ." His emphasis was on *practice*, which by definition indicates our inability to achieve that lofty goal. His experience and teachings are particularly profound because he learned them while working as kitchen help in a monastery. He implores us not to differentiate between secular or sacred but to maintain equal motivation in all things to the glory of God.[6]

Those who attempt to display humility are usually quickly identified as phony and as having little true humility. The truly humble are those who attempt to follow Paul's dictum "not to think of yourself more highly than you ought to think, but to think with sober judgment, each according to the measure of faith that God has assigned" (Rom 12:3).

This kind of thinking does not make for false humility. It does not implore us to put ourselves down or to think we are doormats to be walked on. Instead, it allows us to think rightly of ourselves and to be grateful for the measure of faith God has given us. There's nothing more nauseating than the drama of false humility. By the same token, there's nothing more disgusting than false pride.

How do we attain the proper balance? Thinking rightly is the answer, since thought precedes action. Such thinking promotes integrated memory, and all imitation—including practicing followership of Christ—is predicated on memory from role models, convincing preaching and relationship with those who promote such values. Preaching attends to healing the mind—to healing the imbalance.

How does this happen? Healing of the mind is not a simple process. Some maintain that a light from heaven strikes and everything changes, as with Paul. Maybe this happens with some, but not with most. In truth, maybe it happens with no one. We don't know what Saul was thinking before he became Paul. It's assumed, maybe wrongly, that his intent right up to the moment of conversion was evil. However, the mind is a tricky mechanism. Even while evildoers are in process, they're often in conflict with their inner person. Freud would call this id/superego conflict. Others might maintain that God within us prevents any of us from doing evil without qualms of conscience.

We do know from reliable research that certain brain steps lead to thought and behavioral change. Noted researcher James O. Prochaska outlined six specific stages of change: precontemplation, contemplation, preparation, action, maintenance and termination.[7] These stages are helpful for preachers when viewed as mechanisms for understanding spiritual growth, and for that matter, spiritual conversion.

In the precontemplation stage, change is not intended and may actually be unintended. In the contemplation stage, change is anticipated but "not now." In the preparation stage, some minimal thought and even preliminary action has been taken for the change the person sees as inevitable. In the action stage, recognizable modifications take place. In the maintenance stage, the goal is to prevent relapse. In the termination stage, temptation for return to old thinking and action ceases.

What a wonderful illustration for preachers who wish to heal the brain and mind by instilling spiritual thinking and godly living. Let's look at them one by one in the light of neuropsychological and neurosociological principles.

Precontemplation. Parishioners, especially children and those not accustomed to listening to sermons, may sit seemingly mentally motionless for months or years. This is a period when the minister may feel that sermons are for naught. But the seed is sown, and germination is variable and sometimes unpredictable, depending on many factors, such as rainfall amounts, weed infestation and wind. The same is true of sermon seeds that germinate under many conditions, such as family interference or support, occupational conflicts, educational biases and so on.

Contemplation. This category may at times represent a significant number within any congregation, or for that matter society in general, in regard to lifestyle changes. The studies done for Prochaska's work didn't focus on religious change but on behavioral change, such as cessation of smoking and other harmful habits. However, the principle is adaptable and theologically correct for religious change as well. In the contemplation period, parishioners may become involved in church activities, take on temporary behavioral changes, "try on" a new vocabulary and even make furtive attempts at confession and or conversion. This is a valuable stage for perceptive clergy, since the brain is seeking and experimenting with new ways of believing and practicing faith.

Preparation. This is a crucial stage in the religious-spiritual development of a person. There are both conscious and unconscious processes at work in the brain. Old beliefs are being reexamined, consequences of possible changes are being debated, plans are being made if anticipated changes don't work out, and overt experimentation with new thinking and action is taking place. These people are the most available of all for spiritual growth and for brain-belief and life-faith growth. Their brain believes; and their life functions on faith. They are likely the most ready to receive the preached message.

Action. Unfortunately, many preachers skip the previous steps and spend all their time and energy seeking action from parishioners. It rarely occurs this way, as was discussed in relation to the apostle Paul. Many believe that, in the great revivals, people took action without the previous steps, but we have no proof of such. Certainly the villages of Wales, where the Welsh Revival occurred, were the homes of many great churches, fine hymn singing and many great preachers. In all likelihood, converts attended many services before most converted. From the theological point of view, we know that the Holy Spirit is at work long before we know it and in ways we can't comprehend. We attend to the previous steps faithfully, knowing that fruit will be born in due time.

Maintenance. This happens in the early days of a "new convert," who is attempting to become grounded in the faith and prevent relapse (backsliding) and is still experimenting with his or her newfound lifestyles. Prochaska indicates that "a common reason that people relapse early in action is that they are not well prepared for the prolonged effort needed to progress to maintenance."[8] This statement is especially appropriate for ministers who expect the action step without sufficient attention to the preceding steps. The church has much to offer those in this stage, including congregational support, peer support and pastoral counseling.

For the most part, clergy have shied away from speaking about mental illness, although the Scriptures are replete with illustrations of people suffering from many different forms of mental illness. Today those conditions would be diagnosed and treated. There are many reasons that the church has avoided confrontation with mental illness, including the lack of education regarding the mind and religious ignorance that classifies mental illness as sin or as the "workings of the devil." Many Christians find maintaining the faith difficult, not only due to the nature of the human, but also due to mental conflicts and illnesses of a neuropsychological nature.

Termination. Most Christians probably never reach this stage—the stage of "zero temptation and 100% self-efficacy."[9] In fact, by definition, Christians will never be self-efficient, but will forever rely on spiritual power from the Holy Spirit and the fellowship of believers.

13

Brain Healing and the Body

The Lord will turn away from you every illness.

MOSES (DEUT 7:15)

The body can't be separated from the brain. Psychosomatic medicine offered philosophies and psychologies of body-mind illness before the time of Freud. The brain produces the neural connections that support or discourage the neuroconnections, neurotransmitters and neural-energy for the body to either stay sick or get well. Preaching can play a vital part in allowing and helping the mind as a positive reinforcing agent for health.

The New Testament concept of the physical body is that "we are the temple of the living God" (2 Cor 6:16). Therefore, theologically based preaching requires addressing body health. Ministers do not have to be physiologists or physicians, but powerful, purposeful preaching to heal the body requires a minimal modern understanding of how the body works. Anatomical and physiological knowledge are consistent with spiritual healing—not magic but mystical. Miraculous healing certainly has occurred, does occur and shall continue to occur.

Biblically based belief and preaching do not rest on magic. We must remember that magic is deception and sleight of hand. Mysticism is full of awe and beyond human comprehension. God does not operate by magic, but by mysticism. "For my thoughts are not your thoughts, nor are your ways my ways, says the Lord. For as the heavens are higher than the earth, so are my ways higher than your ways and my thoughts than your thoughts" (Is 55:8-9).

Preaching to the body as well as to the brain/mind is scriptural. Much of Christendom has lost the power of preaching by ignoring Old Testament preaching to the body. Laws regarding diet, sanitation, sexual behavior, personal hygiene and other issues weren't idle words, but were the best living practices of the time—good for all, religious or not. While ignoring Old Testament laws, Christendom gave up paying attention to the body, and preaching to the soul gained supremacy, as if godly living could ignore the body, with its appetites and functions. Christianity in many ways separated soul and body in much the same erroneous fashion as did Descartes with the mind and body. Both are incompatible with the holistic view of the human as taught in both the Old and New Testaments.

As a result, ministers have separated themselves and their messages from many of the life-threatening issues of the day, including anorexia and morbid obesity. Preaching to heal the person requires paying attention to lifestyle—that's what the Levitical law was all about. Not many today would see community sanitation as a spiritual concern, but it is. Dis-ease brings about disease, and disease brings about dis-ease. Both create the foundation for ill health of mind and body.

Let's consider just how the body goes about healing itself:

1. Most prescriptions do not heal but allow for healing by restoring homeostasis within the body.

2. The body musters the resources of the immune system, digestive and elimination processes, hormonal balance and "fighter cells" (T cells) together with environmental and spiritual contributions.

3. The body pulls food from its pantry (sugar, water, protein and so on) for fuel for its power plants (mitochondria—tiny parts of each cell).

4. The body depends on signals from the brain (physical largely from the pituitary; emotional largely from the amygdala, cortex and limbic system) to gain homeostasis, or healing.

Most people discuss the healing process as we have here—from item one to item four—but this is probably backwards, particularly when considering its relevance to preaching. It is necessary to start with the mind (number four) and work backwards. This process then allows a cascade of brain healing to occur.

It isn't sacrilegious or in any way a denial of God's power to recognize the many ways God works. A healing is real, regardless of the methodology of that healing. Nor does it take away from the healing to admit to the complicated, diverse and intertwined factors that caused it. One of these factors is the neuroplasticity of the brain. *Neuroplasticity* is a process in which the neural circuitry in the brain constantly adapts to current needs.

A central dogma of early neuroscience was that the neurons of the adult brain do not change. However, modern neuroscience now recognizes that the brain can reorganize (this reorganization is called "neuroplasticity") throughout life, not only in early childhood. Our brains rewire to create new connections, set out on new paths, and assume new roles.[1]

Newberg asked, "So what does neuroplasticity have to do with God? Everything, for if you contemplate something as complex or mysterious as God, you're going to have incredible bursts of neural activity firing in different parts of your brain."[2]

Although many elements in the brain are more static, neurons and their connections, while relatively permanently positioned anatomically, have properties and functions that are not static. "A single neuron, for instance, has approximately 1,300 presyn-

aptic terminals with which it contacts about twenty-five different
target cells—motor neurons, excitatory interneurons and inhib-
itory interneurons."[3] In other words, the brain's working is far
beyond the most sophisticated human knowledge. Furthermore,
the brain is always changing. It isn't a stagnant system poured in
concrete. It changes rapidly from birth until death. Noted neuroscientist and Nobel laureate Kandel has convincingly demonstrated that we continue to learn as long as our brain is alive.[4]

Again, the mind and body can't be separated. Descartes was
wrong. What is known as the Cartesian philosophy of mind and
body attempted to see the mind as a separate entity from the body,
and vice versa. Descartes's theory, even at that uninformed time,
was so difficult to defend that two of his disciples, Arnold Geulinex
and Nicholas Malebranche, thought very differently, proposing
that all mind/body relationships require a direct intervention from
God. They didn't know how accurate they were in terms of both
theology and neurobiology. Even Descartes revealed his own
doubts in his *Meditations on First Philosophy*.[5]

The search for the soul was evident in all the early philosophers.
Descartes's graphic design of dualism shows how "inputs are
passed on by the sensory organs to the epiphysis in the brain and
from there to what he called an immaterial spirit."[6] The yearning
for truth continues, especially among those who struggle with ambiguity, which Christians know to be *faith*.

The search for the truth, which has been present all along in the
Scriptures, is now ratified by experience and neurobiology. Not
that Christians *need* this ratification, but we now have additional
scientific information to help the unbelieving mind accept the
mysteries of God. And the preacher who understands that God
uses known and unknown physiology and neurobiology for healing
can better address how we believers might respect and treat the
temple of God in which we live.

The concept of healing the body is similar to that of healing the mind; although at times God chooses to act urgently, healing is usually a process. This process is based on the laws of health—some we know, and many we do not yet know. The Old Testament gave great credence to nutrition and healthy living. Although the New Testament doesn't emphasize the laws of food, clothing and health, we must not lose sight of the fact that Jesus told us that he did not come to destroy the law but to fulfill it. We need not destroy it either, but learn from it.

Preachers aren't out of their territory to proclaim proper nutrition, exercise and healthful living. Preachers who are overweight or practice unhealthy lifestyles call attention to their disregard for their temple. Some have likened this to being treated for obesity by a morbidly obese physician or to being advised to give up tobacco by a doctor who smokes.

To preach successfully regarding healing the body, a bit of knowledge about how the body responds to the spoken word is essential. Words are translated into thoughts, and thoughts become brain waves that activate neurophysiological and neurochemical channels. Hormones respond to thoughts and feelings. There is compelling evidence that how we think determines what chemicals are activated. The proverb "For as he thinks in his heart, so is he" (Prov 23:7 Amplified Bible) is not idle information but a solemn warning.

Preaching helps us to think. It has the power to set the stage for healthy thinking. It has the authority of the Scriptures and the church behind it to back up the admonition for godly treatment of the human body. Now as never before, preaching even has the power of neuroscience behind it.

The literature on spirituality and health is voluminous and growing daily. Pseudoreligious organizations, gurus and a wide variety of humanistic healers have assumed the rights for preaching healthful living. Mind/body theories and therapies abound. Very few religious groups have maintained an emphasis on health and healthful living. Seventh-day Adventists, Mormons and Christian Scientists seem to stand alone on this matter. The departure from preaching on bodily health is a serious defect in modern preaching. The federal government, health agencies and the medical world are caught up in how to turn around our unhealthy lifestyles, which result in obesity, heart disease, diabetes and numerous other debilitating diseases. The church should have been holding hands with the medical profession to protect the temple of God.

Neurobiologist Bruce Lipton outlined most cogently how *belief* translates into bodily health and illness. Without debunking the values of modern medicine, he stated,

> I believe that medical education should train doctors to recognize the power of our internal resources. . . . Doctors should not dismiss the power of the mind as something inferior to the power of chemicals and the scalpel. They should let go of their conviction that the body and its parts are essentially stupid and that we need outside intervention to maintain our health.[7]

Lipton might also have said that *ministers* should not dismiss the power of the mind. Ministers speak and leave the rest up to the Holy Spirit. Do we not believe that the Holy Spirit uses preaching to heal the body as much as he uses physicians?

14

Brain Healing and the Community

Behold, how good and how pleasant it is
for brethren to dwell together in unity!

PSALM 133:1 KJV

As old as the book of Proverbs is the statement "As a person thinks, so shall he be." The community can heal only as our brains are rewired to rethink how the values we "say" we hold apply to the larger "self"—that is, the community and nation. Just like individuals and organizations, communities have distinct personalities. These community personalities inherit and develop their own sociological and spiritual illnesses. There's no place on earth where community healing can be more effective than in a pulpit, through a sermon.

The ethic of preaching is not only singular but also plural, and not only individual but also communal; therefore, preaching must speak to the community. We can easily see the need to understand ethics within the context of community, even though we rarely realize the far-reaching effects of preaching—even to those not in attendance. We only have to think about how societies interact to recognize that sermons affect whole communities as a result of social interactions like educational programs and political activities. For instance, think of the far-reaching implications of a sermon heard by many people in a community (but not all) on Jesus and race relations in our public schools, or on what the New Testament teaches regarding taxation. A person does not have to be present to be directly and indirectly affected by what local preachers espouse! The individual and the corporate body must be enjoined to participate together in an active application of ethics to produce a biblical ethos represented by the ethic of the gospel. The individual, the corporate local church membership and the community at large are the end product—the *telos* of the Scriptures.

To reach a better understanding of the end product—the telos— we must first have an adequate understanding of the difference between *ethos, ethic* and *ethics*. Ethos is the very soul and essence of who we are. Ethic is the body of presumed truth from which we operate. Ethics are the ever-changing rules by which we live daily.

Once again, we are confronted with the necessity of understanding the very nature and out-workings of preaching encompassed in the words *ethos, ethic,* and *ethics*. They are all derived from a common source: the Greek word *ēthikos*. Ethos is the fundamental character or spirit of a person, a society or a culture. It's the foundation material of a person, a society or a group. Ethos characterizes and distinguishes the behavior of that individual or group. It's the substance, the matrix, the *ethereal* (*ethe* + *real*) and the *real*. Like ether, another derivative of the same Greek word, *ethos* is an imaginative, tenuous, poetic word that has its root in that light, airy gas that can put us to sleep. However, there is nothing unreal about ethos. We must look at the real and seemingly unreal presentation of it.

As extraneous as it may seem—and admittedly repetitive—the clergy person absolutely must grapple with the very core of *what clergy is, what clergy claims to do and what clergy actually does*. To miss this distinction is to entertain intellectual stimulation that provides nothing more than ego satisfaction. So, once again, give personal, prayerful consideration to understanding a foundational message of this book: the interrelationship yet the essential differences between ethos, ethic and ethics.

- Ethos is the result of accumulated, carefully organized (yet always disorganized), uncontrolled (yet regulated), unconscious (yet conscious) information, tradition and history that is the core being of an individual or organization. Ethos is who you are. It's the basis for all that an individual, group or organization thinks, feels and does.

- Ethic differs from ethos in that it is the body of moral principles derived from ethos. Whereas ethos is often carved in stone, ethic is consciously changeable—which may then in turn have its effect on ethos. Changing an ethic requires our assent and permission to do so.

- Ethics differs from both ethos and ethic. It is the combined elements from ethos out of which we unconsciously choose (or have thrust on us) how to live daily life. It differs from ethic because it deals with the minutia of specifically doing what we do.[1]

At times, the behavior of any given individual or group appears to be a combination of the real and the unreal. Actually this appearance is due to the fact that some aspects of behavior emanate from within, and other aspects are externally superimposed by the regulations (ethics) of the group or by society. It's often difficult for individuals or groups to distinguish even within themselves those beliefs and behaviors that are intrinsically driven and those that are extrinsically demanded. Ethos becomes that accumulated, carefully organized yet disorganized, uncontrolled but regulated sociological part of a culture that gives a corporate image or specific identity to a given subculture. It's the underlying substance that provides the fuel for beliefs, customs and practices. Theology, unique among all disciplines, has the ability to unify ethos, ethic and ethics. In other words, theology defines what is, what it claims to be and what it does.

Powerful preaching understands that we constantly strive to gain conformity between what we really are, what we purport to be and what we are seen to be by others. Further, preaching that plans for a positive outcome demonstrates a growing congruence of these realities; the end result is the telos. Purposeful preaching presumes to tackle the problem of life/spirit incongruity by specifically and intentionally offering methods for rectifying this disparity. Life and spirit rarely coincide. What we wish is often not what we do, and what we do is often not what we wish. The apostle Paul was quite clear in his own confession of this (Rom 7:15).

Preaching includes, but is not limited to, developing the life of a congregation, which includes the sacraments, plus encouraging better spiritual thinking. The concept of telos may help us to understand the awesome responsibility that comes with the power of preaching. Telos is the end product: in education, it is the graduate; in religion, it is the convert. What product are we expecting from a sermon? What is the *real*, though unspoken, motive behind our preaching? What is the product we are attempting to produce? We must strive for a telos that is intellectually solid, morally sound, theologically grounded and biblically accurate. This meets the criteria of being for the greater good of all who hear, meeting the requirements for aligning ethics with ethic.

Preaching to pet projects and rearranging Scripture to bolster unique, individualized ideologies is not to the greater good. The end product will be defective, and the listeners will continue to act in contradiction to ethic. In such instances, congregations become warriors for insignificant or even the wrong causes, carrying a banner other than Christ's. The unbelieving world sees the discrepancy between our ethics (what we do) and our ethic (who we say we are). Congregants hear the words but not the message, which then escapes becoming part of the Christian telos.

Words take on meaning, and thus appeal to those willing to hear, only when backed by authority. From early childhood, the brain is constantly asking, "Why should I believe that?" to which this glib answer frequently is given by a parent: "Because I say so." Only because the parent has authority does the child consider accepting the information. The Scriptures are full of "Thus saith the Lord"— which is God saying, "Because I say so."

PREACHING WITH AUTHORITY PIERCES THE ARMOR

We are enjoined by Jesus and all Christian theology to work toward healing relationships between denominations, churches and groups inside and outside the Christian community *without* compromising individual theological belief systems. There has never been a more appropriate time for those who profess to follow the teachings of Jesus Christ to sing "Blest Be the Tie That Binds." In the past, it was often believed that communities could live and let live by isolating themselves in denominations, religious orders and other organizational structures. In those days, the song was "Blest Be the Tie That *Blinds*." Denominational differences became barriers to fellowship when even the smallest points of theological belief or ecclesiastical practice differed. The church will survive— in some form. It has done so over the ages, during times of equal or even greater obstacles. However, that's no excuse for being indifferent about its survival or for repeating history.

More and more, new congregations are either joining no denomination or maintaining a very low profile in a denomination by emphasizing that they are a community church. Denominations have been disappointing to many parishioners, who are tired of denominational sermons, harangues for denominationally determined financial matters, denominational spending for purposes that they have little or no interest in supporting and denominational ties that promote the denomination more than the gospel message. Denominations are represented as communities, but often this is not clearly felt by members. Congregants complain that, although fellowship and community are offered within the local congregations, there is very little actual relational support or knowledge of what goes on in the lives of their community of believers. Small-group organizations inside and outside the church are offering many parishioners a truer relationship than the church does.

The community is not restricted to the congregated body called the local church. We are not exempt from doing all we can to heal all communities. Five major, recognized social institutions are defined below, and we aren't relieved of duty toward any of them. In the light of ethos, ethic and ethics, we must vigorously examine our *being*, our *intent* and our *action*. In the light of these guidelines, we must honestly evaluate the outcomes.

- The educational institution—schools, colleges, universities. Many of these have fallen into spiritual disrepair. The Christian must ask if those who profess Christ and teach in such places, those who serve on boards, those who go and whose children go to those institutions are doing all they can to turn the tide in education. Preaching to educators regarding the necessity of healing within the educational community is our responsibility.

- The domestic institution—family, parents, brothers, sisters, in-laws, relatives of all generations. Healing is greatly needed. Reports are now common of immediate family members, even parents and children, who no longer speak to each other.

- The political institutions—legislators, the president, judges, courts and the legal system. It would take more than one book to cite the grave danger our country faces if the political system continues its downward spiral regarding human injustice, corruption, graft and dishonesty.

- The religious institution—local congregations, denominations, mission boards, seminaries, Bible schools, religious publishing companies, religious broadcasters and ancillary Christian organizations. Abuses lie in such practices as pushing denominationalism at the expense of the gospel, bleeding money from listeners and subscribers under questionable pretenses, and the misuse of both money and influence. Some offenders are wolves in sheep's clothing, and particularly the trusting elderly population falls prey to them.

• The financial institution—banks, credit unions, insurance companies, mutual funds, credit card companies. How would we even begin to describe the need for moral reform in our corrupt, thievery-ridden financial organizations?

Some would argue that the church should stick to the gospel and stay out of social issues. Only those who have not read or refuse to follow the dictum of the Old Testament prophets, the Sermon on the Mount and the writings of Paul dare to say such things. The prophets railed against the sins of the organizations of the day, and Jesus drove a financial institution's representatives out of the temple. How much more dramatic would the Scriptures have to be about our Christian responsibility for the dysfunctional yet organized world in which we live? The preacher doesn't have to minimize the gospel to preach about the healing of communities—all of them. Communities are made up of individuals to whom the preacher can minister and whose lives can change. Neighborhoods, cities and nations can be redeemed one person at a time and occasionally in groups.

Healing the community requires great care, drastic changes and more risk than the church may be willing to take. Traditional ways of doing things may have to give way to newer methods that cost less money, require more participation and demand a greater degree of commitment than today's Christians are willing to give. And there may be backlash. Dietrich Bonhoeffer's *The Cost of Discipleship* paints a picture in vivid colors that most of us don't want on our palette. He was hanged at thirty-nine for a kind of commitment we may be called on to make if the church is to be saved and reconciled to the ever more secularized and politicized demands being placed on it.

Bonhoeffer was a preacher, and his preaching served as his multicolored palette. Discipleship allows reconciliation, and only through preaching will the recognition necessary to reengage the brain and require new commitment be possible. Preaching is the communicating element for accomplishing this part of healing.

Preaching to heal the community doesn't start with feeding the hungry, housing the homeless and clothing the poor—although it certainly includes them. It must start with healing the soul of the community. Feeding, housing and clothing are some of the methods of this healing. But before the methods can be effective, there must be prepared givers and prepared receivers. A prepared giver is defined as "whoever gives you a cup of water to drink because you bear the name of Christ will by no means lose the reward" (Mk 9:41).

We asked a question in the beginning of this book: "How is the church different from any other social agency?" This is the answer. This is the critical and essential difference between a social service agency, such as the Red Cross, and the church. The work of social agencies is undoubtedly good, and even godly. But the church can offer not only physical sustenance but also sustenance of the soul. The prepared giver is the true missionary. The prepared receiver is the true disciple. The prepared giver and the prepared receiver are both the prepared blessed.

The church often ignores the Great Commission: "Go therefore and make disciples of all nations, baptizing them in the name of the Father and of the Son and of the Holy Spirit, and teaching them to obey everything that I have commanded you" (Mt 28:19-20). If not, often the first part of this requirement is emphasized sufficiently. The latter part is where the preaching comes in. It's not enough to "make disciples"—that is, to convert others to the faith; it's obligatory to teach them to obey everything that has been commanded, which includes the Sermon on the Mount and the entire message of God's redemption through Jesus Christ.

The recipient who is prepared to receive is also special. She or he is not simply one who accepts a gift. Christian psychiatrist Paul Tournier wrote an entire book on gifts, called *The Meaning of Gifts* (1986). Gifts aren't without purpose, and they aren't without *overt* and *covert* messages. The prepared receiver understands that although the human giver makes no demands on the receiver, receiving the gift engenders gratitude and thanksgiving in the recipient's heart. Further, that heart may become prepared only after receiving the gift. No one can accept a gift without feeling the necessity to reciprocate in some way. A simple thank-you is the verbal response, but the gift lives on. Each time the gift is seen, tasted, touched, felt or smelled, the relationship that has been built between two people doing God's work is kindled once more.

We are the recipients and therefore ones who are, by the very nature of the gift, enjoined—not required—to pass on the gift. This is not obligation; it is relationship. Relationship results from evidenced love. Giving in the name of Christ, who gave to us, is the symbolic and very tangible preaching of the Word.

To preach by wooing (reward) or to preach woe (judgment) is the critical question facing the preacher who wishes to reach the community. The concept of reward (woo) and punishment (woe) was well established long before Pavlov (1849–1936) demonstrated it in his famous experiments on classical conditioning, though he won the Nobel Prize in 1904 for his work.

> He conducted an experiment in which he rang a bell just prior to administering food to the dog. At first, the dog showed no particular reaction to the bell. But after several trials in which the dog heard the bell just before eating, he began to salivate in response to the bell alone . . . what had originally been a neutral stimulus now controlled the dog's salivation.[2]

Skinner (1904–1990) extended these experiments to show the results of "operant conditioning," in which he proved how it "can be used to shape a brand new response, which the organism would never exhibit if left on its own."[3]

Both of these psychologists, and many other researchers performed experiments that demonstrated the effects of reward and punishment. Sometimes the avoidance of punishment is in itself reward. In all cases, the pain of woe is gladly exchanged for the reward from woo, even when considerable work is required to obtain the reward. In all cases, reinforcement is continuously required, just as the children of Israel needed to be reminded of the commandments the Lord had given to them.

This concept was known and practiced effectively in ancient civilizations and the Old Testament is replete with woe (judgment/punishment). Although the term *woe* is found in the New Testament, it's most often found within a context referring back to the Old Testament. To be certain, there is some balance between woe and woo in both the Old and New Testaments, but the concept of grace, which is the higher definition of *woo*, is a New Testament concept altogether. The "grace" of the Old Testament was the hypothesis: avoid evil and reward will result. This "earned" reward is not comparable to the New Testament concept of grace. Although we are certainly admonished to avoid evil, we earn grace by avoiding evil. To obtain grace, we live in grace, which enables us to avoid evil.

The New Testament concept of grace, or being blessed (rewarded), is that it is unmerited and can't be earned. Further, because of the loving nature of God, it can't be avoided. This idea that grace can't be avoided is often overlooked. The grace of God, by definition, is only his to give; we have no part in it for ourselves or for others. We can extend our grace but not his. We can love to our fullest ability, but God may choose to bestow grace upon those we find difficult (or impossible) to love. We might write the following words differently if we were to write the Scriptures, but they're mighty clear verses:

> You have heard that it was said, "You shall love your neighbor and hate your enemy." But I say to you, Love your enemies and pray for those who persecute you, so that you may be children of your Father in heaven; for he makes his sun rise on the evil and on the good, and sends rain on the righteous and on the unrighteous. (Mt 5:43-45)

Woe conjures up thoughts of draconian results, otherwise known as severe punishment. Certainly we can't read the Scriptures and avoid the concept of judgment and punishment for evil, but the Christian message differs significantly from that of the Old Testament in its emphasis on God's provision of grace in spite of human frailty. Our job is not to see how many people can fall so we can show that we are able to pick them up, but rather to keep them from falling in the first place. For example, we don't shove a child in front of a moving vehicle to show that we can jump in and be a savior. Rather, by modeling, we show others how to avoid the "punishment" that would result from such behavior.

There's such a thing as "tough love." Love without justice may not in fact be love. Although many modern-day preachers might disagree with Jonathan Edwards's famous sermon "Sinners in the Hands of an Angry God," we can readily see that his motive was to woo by way of threatening woe. But this may not be the approach that fits our communities today.

We teach and practice the positive because we wish to avoid pain and punishment, and we have learned through many generations of experimentation that reward comes from proper behavior. Therefore, we feed the hungry, house the homeless and care for the sick—not *only* so they should not be hungry, homeless or sick, but also so the message of grace wins.

It's important for us to recognize the difference between pun-

ishment and discipline. Discipline may involve negative consequences for wrongful behavior, but the goal is not to punish but to
disciple. Certainly we can't read Jesus' words without recognizing
the intentionality of making disciples rather than of meting out
punishment.

To put this section in proper perspective, we only need to look
again at the scriptural admonition found in the Great Commission:
"Go therefore and make disciples of all nations, baptizing them in
the name of the Father and of the Son and of the Holy Spirit, and
teaching them to obey everything that I have commanded you.
And remember, I am with you always, to the end of the age" (Mt
28:19-20).

Dénouement and Benediction

This dénouement is not an ending but a blessing on a beginning. So it is with the sermon and with this book. The purpose is not to give a "completion" but a challenge that can't be ignored and must be continued.

A dénouement is the final resolution or statement of the position presented; therefore, this is the final argument for a total healing within the church, starting with positive, powerful, purposeful preaching. The church may well be at a crossroad similar to that experienced in former days—days of persecution, days of exclusion, days of ecclesiastical unrest and days when it went underground for survival. As an organization, the church faces challenges that this generation has not experienced. Can the church survive? Many say no. Others debate whether it should in its present form. The church universal need not fear, for Jesus said, "On this rock I will build my church, and the gates of Hades will not prevail against it" (Mt 16:18).

There are many rocks on which the church is being built, and local congregations have much to consider and reconsider. Preaching has never lost its power, but many preachers have. It has been abundantly demonstrated through history, throughout the Scriptures (both Old and New Testaments), throughout worldwide missionary endeavors and now through the latest neuroscientific discoveries that preaching works. Preaching must once again be elevated to a position of prominence. We know both *that* it works and *why* it works.

A benediction is not an end, nor is it the end of this book. It is the blessing that sends forth the message of this book and an encouragement that promotes preaching powerful, purposeful sermons that produce positive results.

Now to God who is able to strengthen you according to my gospel and the proclamation of Jesus Christ, according to the revelation of the mystery that was kept secret for long ages but is now disclosed, and through the prophetic writings is made known to all the Gentiles, according to the command of the eternal God, to bring about the obedience of faith—to the only wise God, through Jesus Christ, to whom be the glory forever! Amen. (Rom 16:25-27)

Gloria in excelsis Deo!

Acknowledgments

This book would not be complete without thanking the many persons who have forced it into reality. Parishioners, patients, friends and, most of all, family have caused me to ponder and eventually put into writing many convictions that have come from now nearly a lifetime of ministry. I especially want to thank my wife; without her patience and partnership such a life could not have been lived. Special thanks is also more than deserved by Al Hsu and his staff at InterVarsity Press, who have corrected so much of my otherwise faulty writing style.

Appendix

Checklist for Sermon Preparation

Does this sermon

- excite me and propel me in a specific direction?
- change, affirm or reaffirm my beliefs?
- provide foundation material for all listeners to "tie back to" (*religare*)?
- offer multiple brain gates that help those of all ages and educational backgrounds to understand?
- lay the foundation for subsequent pastoral care?
- provide a peak experience for the worship service?
- prepare the way for the next sermon?

Notes

PREFACE

[1]Charles Haddon Spurgeon, *Lectures to My Students* (Grand Rapids: Zondervan, 1954), p. 413.

[2]*The Works of John Wesley*, vol. 10 (1872; repr., Grand Rapids: Zondervan, 1958), p. 483.

[3]Ibid., p. 484.

CHAPTER 1: A BRAINSTORM VERSUS A SHORT CIRCUIT

[1]Andrew Newberg and Mark Waldman, *How God Changes Your Brain* (New York: Ballantine, 2009), pp. 6-7.

[2]Ibid., p. 43.

[3]Ibid., pp. 43-44.

CHAPTER 2: LINKING BRAIN AND SERMON

[1]Richard Lischner, *A Theology of Preaching* (Eugene, Ore.: Wipf & Stock, 2001), p. 78.

[2]Daniel Levitin, *This Is Your Brain on Music* (New York: Plume, 2007), p. 197.

[3]Stephen Duggan, *A Student's Textbook in the History of Education*, 3rd ed. (New York: Appleton-Century-Crofts, 1948), pp. 222-42.

[4]Ibid., p. 476.

[5]Ray Jackendoff, *Foundations of Language* (Oxford, UK: Oxford University Press, 2002), p. 162.

[6]Benedict Carey, "Studying Young Minds, and How to Teach Them," *New York Times*, December 21, 2009, p. A-1.

[7]Karl Rahner, *Encyclopedia of Theology: The Concise Sacramentum Mundi* (New York: Crossroad, 1975), p. 1359.

[8]Ibid.

[9]George Arthur Buttrick, Keith George and Crim Butterick, eds., *The Interpreter's Dictionary of the Bible*, vol. 3 (Nashville: Abingdon, 1962), p. 808.

[10]Louis Cozolino, *The Neuroscience of Psychotherapy* (New York: Norton, 2002), p. 35.

[11]Ernest Rossi, *The Psychobiology of Mind-Body Healing*, quoted in ibid., p. 37.

[12]Norman Doidge, *The Brain That Changes Itself* (New York: Penguin, 2007), p. 63.

[13]Ibid., pp. 64-70.

[14]Raymond Corsini, *The Dictionary of Psychology* (Albany, Calif.: Taylor & Francis, 1999), p. 546.

[15]Huston Smith, *Why Religion Matters* (San Francisco: Harper, 2001), pp. 197-98.

[16]Buttrick, George and Butterick, *Interpreter's Dictionary of the Bible*, p. 868. Also Joseph Thayer, *A Greek-English Lexicon of the New Testament* (New York: American Book, 1889), p. 346.

[17]Thayer, *Greek-English Lexicon,* p. 346.

[18]C. S. Lewis, *Shepherd's Notes on C. S. Lewis's Mere Christianity* (Nashville: Holman Reference, 1999), p. 76.

[19]Andrew Newberg, *Why We Believe What We Believe* (New York: Free Press, 2006), p. 75.

CHAPTER 3: THE BRAIN SEES PREACHING AS UNIQUE

[1]Richard Lischer, *A Theology of Preaching* (Eugene, Ore.: Wipf & Stock, 1992), p. 79.

[2]Michael Werthman, *The Psychology Primer* (Del Mar, Calif.: Publisher's Inc., 1975), p. 39.

[3]The word *engram* is defined by *Webster's Encyclopedic Unabridged Dictionary* as "a durable mark caused by a stimulus upon protoplasm" (*Webster's Encyclopedic Unabridged Dictionary of the English Language,* Updated and Revised Deluxe Edition, s.v. "engram"). This definition fits our discussion admirably since we are asserting the power of what we hear (the stimulus) to embed itself indelibly in our brains.

[4]Norman Doidge, *The Brain That Changes Itself* (New York: Penguin, 2007), p. 301.

[5]Robert Rieber and Aaron Carton, *The Collected Works of L. S. Vygotsky,* vol. 1 (New York: Plenum Press, 1987), pp. 82-83, 173-79.

[6]Raymond Corsini, *The Dictionary of Psychology* (Albany, Calif.: Taylor & Francis, 1999), p. 640.

[7]Andrew Newberg, *Why We Believe What We Believe* (New York: Free Press, 2006), p. 116.

[8]Daniel Levitin, *This Is Your Brain on Music* (New York: Plume, 2007), p. 223.

[9]Thomas Verny, *The Secret Life of the Unborn Child* (New York: Dell, 1981), p. 33.

[10]Newberg, *Why We Believe What We Believe,* p. 125.

[11]Based on Richard Cox, Betty Ervin-Cox and Louis Hoffman, eds., *Spirituality and Psychological Health* (Colorado Springs: Colorado School of Professional Psychology, 2005), pp. 33-56.

[12]*Webster's Encyclopedic Unabridged Dictionary of the English Language,* Updated and Revised Deluxe Edition, s.v. "engram."

CHAPTER 4: THE BRAIN USES PREACHING FOR HEALING

[1]Richard Lischer, *A Theology of Preaching* (Eugene, Ore.: Wipf & Stock, 1992), p. 79.

[2]Richard Lischer, ed., *Theories of Preaching: Selected Readings in the Homiletical Tradition* (Durham, N.C.: Labyrinth Press, 1987), p. 343; see Karl Barth, *The Preaching of the Gospel.*

[3]*Webster's New World College Dictionary,* 4th ed. (New York: Wiley, 2005), p. 1651.

[4]James Orr, gen. ed., *The International Standard Bible Encyclopedia,* vol. 5 (Grand Rapids: Eerdmans, 1949), p. 3110.

[5]*Webster's New World College Dictionary* (New York: Wiley, 2005), p. 132.

[6]Vergilius Ferm, *The Encyclopedia of Religion* (New York: The Philosophical Library, 1945), p. 270.

[7]Ibid.

[8]John Suk, "A Friend in Jesus," *The Christian Century* 128, no. 18 (2011): p. 22.

[9]Andrew Newberg, *Why We Believe What We Believe* (New York: Free Press, 2006), pp. 167-90.

CHAPTER 5: THE CORE PROCESS OF PREACHING IS BRAIN WORK

[1]Jeremiah Loch, *Healing the Whole Person* (New York: Mercy House, 2006), p. 16.

[2]Carl G. Jung, *The Archetypes and the Collective Unconscious,* ed. H. Read (Princeton: Princeton University Press, 1969), p. 43.

CHAPTER 6: PREACHING PROVIDES BRAIN ENERGY

[1]Ursula Anderson, *Taking Out the Violence: Shedding Light on the Science and Soul of Human Behavior* (Sussex, UK: Book Guild, 2003).

[2]Beth Azar, "More Powerful Persuasion," *Monitor* 4 (April 2010): 36.

[3]George Arthur Buttrick, Keith George and Crim Butterick, eds., *The Interpreter's Dictionary of the Bible*, vol. 3 (Nashville: Abingdon, 1962), p. 868.

CHAPTER 7: BRAIN STIMULI PRODUCE BEHAVIORAL RESPONSES

[1]John Buchanan, "Preaching for a Decision," *The Christian Century,* September 28, 2011, accessed at www.christiancentury.org/article/2911-09/preaching-decision.

[2]Eric Kandel, *In Search of Memory* (New York: Norton, 2006), p. 210.

CHAPTER 8: PREACHING AND PASTORING ARE DIFFERENT

[1]Thomas Long, "Why Sermons Bore Us," *The Christian Century,* September 6, 2011, p. 31.

[2]Keith Drury, "21 Skills of Great Preachers," *TuesdayColumn.com* (blog), 1996, http://www.drurywriting.com/keith/preacher.htm. Used with permission.

[3]Mitch Albom, *Have a Little Faith: A True Story* (New York: Hyperion, 2009), p. 7.

[4]John Stauffer, *Giants* (New York: Grand Central Publishers, 2008), p. 87.

[5]Long, "Why Sermons Bore Us," p. 31.

CHAPTER 9: GETTING TO THE BRAIN WITH THEOLOGY

[1]George Washington Hunter, *The Holy Eucharist and Auricular Confession* (London: James McCauley, 1879), p. 83.

[2]Hans Kung, *Freud and the Problem of God* (New Haven, Conn.: Yale University Press, 1979), p. 18.

[3]Raymond Corsini, *The Dictionary of Psychology* (Philadelphia: Brunner/Mazel, 1999), p. 3.

[4]*Webster's Encyclopedic Unabridged Dictionary of the English Language,* Updated and Revised Deluxe Edition, s.v. "repent."

[5]W. T. Stead, *The Story of the Awakening: The Story of the Welsh Revival* (New York: Revell, 1905), p. 62.

[6]Herbert Benson, *Timeless Healing* (New York: Scribner, 1996), p. 183.

[7]André Virel, *Decorated Man: The Human Body as Art* (New York: Abrams, 1980), p. 12.

[8]Ashley Montagu, *Touching: The Significance of the Skin* (New York: Harper & Row, 1971), p. 29.

[9]William A. Tiller, *Science and Human Transformation: Subtle Energies, Intentionality and Consciousness* (Walnut Creek, Calif.: Pavior Publications, 1997), p. 1.

[10]Larry Dossey, *Prayer Is Good Medicine* (San Francisco: Harper, 1996), p. 27.

[11]Ibid., p. 147.

[12]Andrew Newberg and Mark Waldman, *How God Changes Your Brain* (New York: Ballantine, 2009), p. 41.

[13]David H. Bauslin, *The International Standard Bible Encyclopedia,* vol. 4 (Grand Rapids: Eerdmans, 1915), p. 2434.

[14]Ibid.

[15]Laurie Lundy-Ekman, *Neuroscience: Fundamentals for Rehabilitation,* 3rd ed. (St. Louis, Mo.: W. B. Saunders, 2007), p. 72.

[16]George Arthur Buttrick, Keith R. Crim, eds., *The Interpreter's Dictionary of the Bible,* vol. 2 (Nashville: Abingdon, 1955), p. 22.

CHAPTER 10: PREACHING AND THE BRAIN IN PAIN
[1]Evelyn Hutt et al., "Optimizing Pain Management in Long-term Care Residents," 2007, www.medscape.com/viewarticle/564630; and Richard Cox and Sharon Bell, "Neurobiopsychological Approach to Treatment" (paper presented at the Fall Symposium of the Arizona Geriatrics Society, October 29–30, 2010).
[2]F. Agnesi et al., "Wireless Instantaneous Neurotransmitter Concentration System-Based Amperometric Detection of Dopamine, Adenosine, and Glutamate for Intraoperative Neurochemical Monitoring," Journal of Neurosurgery 111, no. 4 (2009): 701-11.
[3][AQ: Is this ibid.?]
[4]Beth Azar, "More Powerful Persuasion," Monitor 4 (April 2010): 36.

CHAPTER 11: BRAIN HEALING AND THE SOUL
[1]Bruce Lipton, The Biology of Belief (Santa Rosa, Calif.: Elite Books, 2005), p. 188.
[2]Ibid., p. 62.
[3]Summa Theologica, quoted in Bertrand Russell, A History of Western Philosophy (New York: Simon & Schuster, 1945), p. 458.
[4]Quoted in Douglas Hofstadter and Daniel Dennett, The Mind's I: Fantasies and Reflections on Self and Soul (New York: Basic Books, 1981), p. 35.
[5]Gary Zukav, The Seat of the Soul (New York: Simon & Schuster, 1989).
[6]Richard Cox, The Sacrament of Psychology (Sanford, Fla.: InSync Press, 2002), p. 109.
[7]Quoted in ibid., p. 111.
[8]Ibid., p. 110.
[9]Harvey Cox, The Future of Faith (New York: HarperCollins, 2009), p. 40.
[10]Susanne Katherina Langer, Philosophy in a New Key (Cambridge, Mass.: Harvard University Press, 1963), p. 47.
[11]Cox, The Sacrament of Psychology, p. 111.
[12]Ibid., p. 145.

CHAPTER 12: BRAIN HEALING AND THE MIND
[1]Raymond Corsini, The Dictionary of Psychology (Philadelphia: Brunner/Mazel, 1999), p. 597.
[2]Ibid.
[3]Geoffrey W. Bromiley, gen. ed., The International Standard Bible Encyclopedia, vol. 3 (Grand Rapids: Eerdmans, 1986), p. 2056.
[4]Ibid.
[5]"Mayo Clinic Researchers Show Brain Waves Can 'Write' on a Computer in Early Tests," December 6, 2009, http://www.mayoclinic.org/news2009-jax/5538.html.
[6]Brother Lawrence, Project Gutenberg, Lightheart, Edit.10, 2002.
[7]James O. Prochaska, Heart and Soul of Change, ed. M. Hubble, B. Duncan and S. Miller (Washington, D.C.: American Psychological Association, 1999), pp. 227-36.
[8]Ibid., p. 231.
[9]Ibid., p. 232.

CHAPTER 13: BRAIN HEALING AND THE BODY
[1]Mario Beauregard and Denyse O'Leary, The Spiritual Brain (New York: Harper, 2007), p. 103.
[2]Ibid., p. 16.
[3]Eric Kandel, In Search of Memory (New York: Norton, 2006), p. 215.
[4]Ibid.

[5]Ibid., p. 135.

[6]Ibid.

[7]Bruce Lipton, *The Biology of Belief* (Santa Rosa, Calif.: Elite Books, 2005), pp. 137-38.

CHAPTER 14: BRAIN HEALING AND THE COMMUNITY

[1]Based on Richard Cox, *Issues of the Soul* (Eugene, Ore.: Resource Publications, 2010).

[2]Michael Werthman, *The Psychology Primer* (Del Mar, Calif.: Publisher's Inc., 1975), pp. 56-59.

[3]Ibid., pp. 63-69.

IVP PRAXIS
EQUIPPING LEADERS FOR MINISTRY

God has called us to ministry. But it's not enough to have a vision for ministry if you don't have the practical skills for it. Nor is it enough to do the work of ministry if what you do is headed in the wrong direction. We need both vision *and* expertise for effective ministry. We need *praxis*.

Praxis puts theory into practice. It brings cutting-edge ministry expertise from visionary practitioners. You'll find sound biblical and theological foundations for ministry in the real world, with concrete examples for effective action and pastoral ministry. Praxis books are more than the "how to" – they're also the "why to." And because *being* is every bit as important as *doing*, Praxis attends to the inner life of the leader as well as the outer work of ministry. Feed your soul, and feed your ministry.

If you are called to ministry, you know you can't do it on your own. Let Praxis provide the companions you need to equip God's people for life in the kingdom.

www.ivpress.com/praxis